VAN GOGH

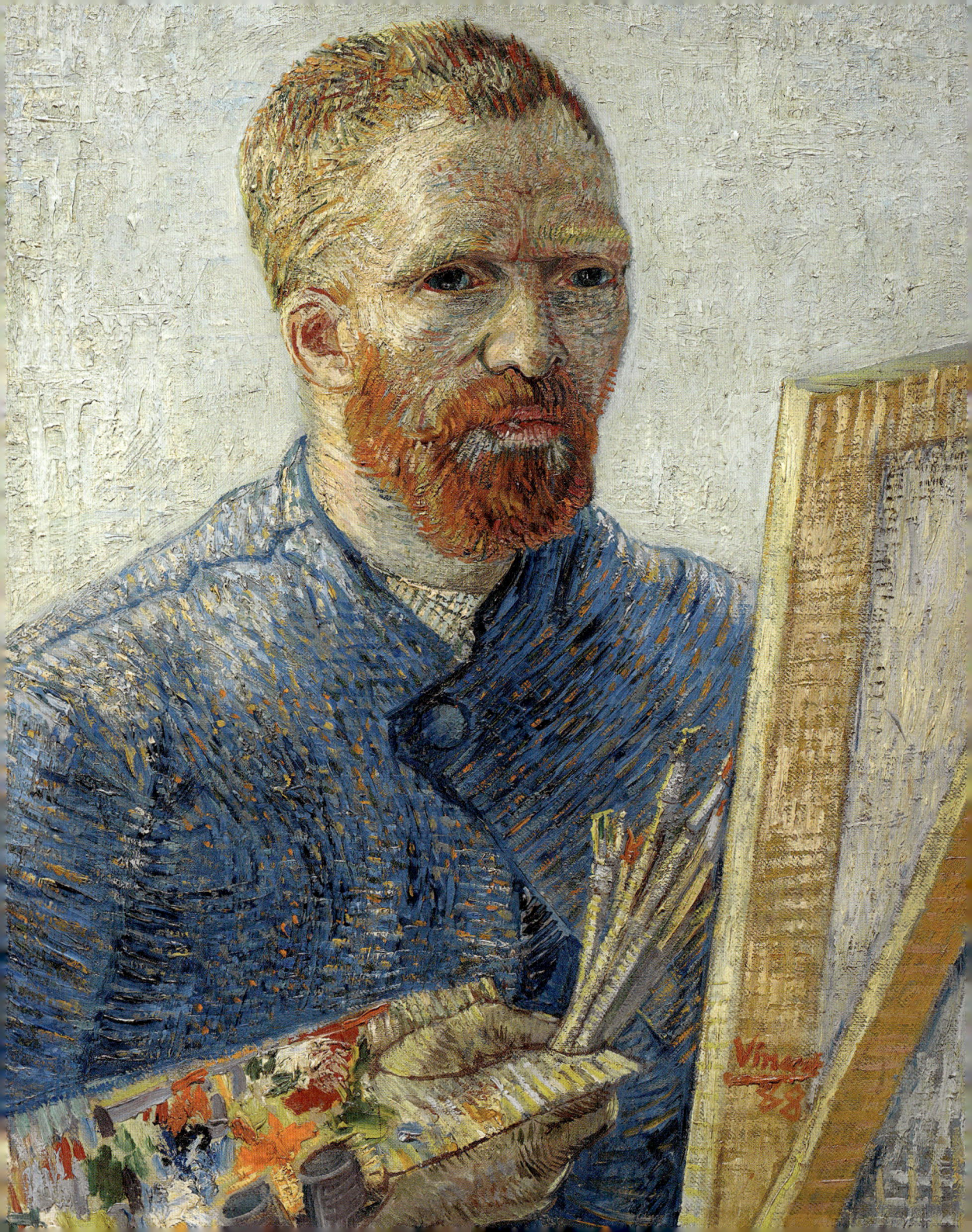

MASTERS OF ART

VAN GOGH

Isabel Kuhl

PRESTEL
Munich · London · New York

Front Cover: Vincent van Gogh, *Sunflowers*,
1888, Neue Pinakothek, Munich (detail, see page 75)

Frontispiece: Vincent van Gogh, *Self-Portrait as a Painter*, 1887/88,
Van Gogh Museum, Amsterdam

© Prestel Verlag, Munich · London · New York 2026
A member of Penguin Random House Verlagsgruppe GmbH
Neumarkter Strasse 28 · 81673 Munich

1st edition 2026

produktsicherheit@penguinrandomhouse.de
(The above information is mandatory information according to GPSR and should be
used for all queries relating to the safety of our books)

A CIP catalogue record for this book is available from the British Library.

Editorial direction, Prestel: Cornelia Hübler
Translation: Russell Stockman
Copyediting and proofreading: Vanessa Magson-Mann, So to Speak, Icking
Production management: Martina Effaga, Cilly Klotz
Design: Florian Frohnholzer, Sofarobotnik
Typesetting: ew print & media service gmbh
Separations: Reproline mediateam
Printing and binding: Livonia Print, Riga
Typeface: Cera Pro
Paper: 150 g/m² Magno Matt

FSC
www.fsc.org
MIX
Paper | Supporting
responsible forestry
FSC® C002795

Penguin Random House Verlagsgruppe FSC® N001967

Printed in Latvia

ISBN 978-3-7913-9312-4

www.prestel.com

CONTENTS

INTRODUCTION

Vincent van Gogh's artistic career spanned a mere ten years. In this short amount of time he not only produced a varied and masterly oeuvre, he also accomplished an impressive change in his painting style, his colouring and his subject matter. And yet van Gogh was a largely self-taught draughtsman and painter. The man who produced the long since world-famous sunflowers and starry nights was essentially an autodidact who turned to art only relatively late: in the 1870s the young Vincent first worked as an art dealer, then as a supply teacher. He ultimately hoped to study theology and become a preacher: Then, after his career plans had been dashed, in 1880 he wagered everything on becoming an artist. To that end he began to draw almost excessively, later to paint as well, mainly motifs from his Dutch homeland in earthy, dark colours—referring to himself as a peasant painter.

But when at thirty van Gogh moved to Paris he abruptly changed his style and his palette. From Montmartre he immersed himself in the city's art world, became familiar with modern art at lightning speed and truly got started. In the next five years he painted all the works that would make him so famous, the *Terrace of a Café at Night*, *The Starry Night*, portraits in radiant colours, pictures of almond blossoms and again and again lush bouquets of sunflowers. While capturing Parisian and somewhat later Provençal motifs in bright colours he frequently felt isolated and was almost always short of money. He suffered worsening health and took care of himself, if at all, only so as to be able to keep painting. When van Gogh took his own life in 1890 he left behind an impressive oeuvre of more than 900 paintings and roughly 1,000 drawings and sketches. It is incomprehensible that all these were produced in only a decade.

Many of Vincent van Gogh's picture motifs have meanwhile become almost ubiquitous, confronting us on calendar pages and coffee cups; others have been virtually forgotten. The present volume includes a selection of famous and less familiar pictures and drawings that reflect van Gogh's development—all of them fascinating. As the selection shows, van Gogh mastered a variety of genres: he drew and painted landscapes most of all, at the same time experimenting time and again with new artistic approaches in his still lifes and he had a special fondness for figural painting. And when van Gogh lacked models, as was most often the case, he painted himself. No fewer than thirty-six self-portraits survive. He captured himself on canvas for the first time shortly after his arrival in Paris and it was only a few years later that he painted his last, remarkable self-portraits. These were done after he had withdrawn to the Saint-Paul-de-Mausole asylum. The ruthlessness with which he analysed himself has helped to nourish the myths about his life: the man who sacrificed everything for painting, the starving artist denied all recognition but whose works after his much too early death sold for record prices—such is the incomplete and distorted story of his brief life.

The solitary genius driven to madness by adverse circumstances and an uncontrollable temperament—this image has long persisted. Yet the notion of an unrecognised artist slaving delusionally at his easel has gradually been abandoned. Much has meanwhile become known about the clarity and determination with which van Gogh produced his art. He himself contradicts the sensational legends that have clustered around his life; the artist's correspondence, especially from the last years of his life, underscores how judiciously and purposefully he viewed his own work. As it happens, van Gogh was not only an unbelievably productive painter but also an articulate correspondent: at least 900 of the letters he wrote to family and friends survive. The great majority were written to his four-years-younger brother Theo. The two corresponded all their lives. The earliest known letter to Theo dates from September 1872, when Vincent was nineteen and apprenticing as an art dealer. When he finally turned to painting, his letters also become illustrated. He frequently included sketches of his works, either on separate sheets or between the lines. He thereby kept Theo, his family and his artist friends up to date in letters, explaining to them his picture concepts as well the state of his constitution. He stayed in contact with painter friends all his life and the link with his family was maintained through his brother. In his letters he emphasises again and again that he is aware of what a difficult path he has chosen with painting. Yet even in his last days there is no trace of the tragic insanity so commonly attributed to this unique artist—and to the man who at the start of his painting career was already fully conscious of its demands: "So much is required that painting today is practically a crusade, a military campaign, a battle or war."

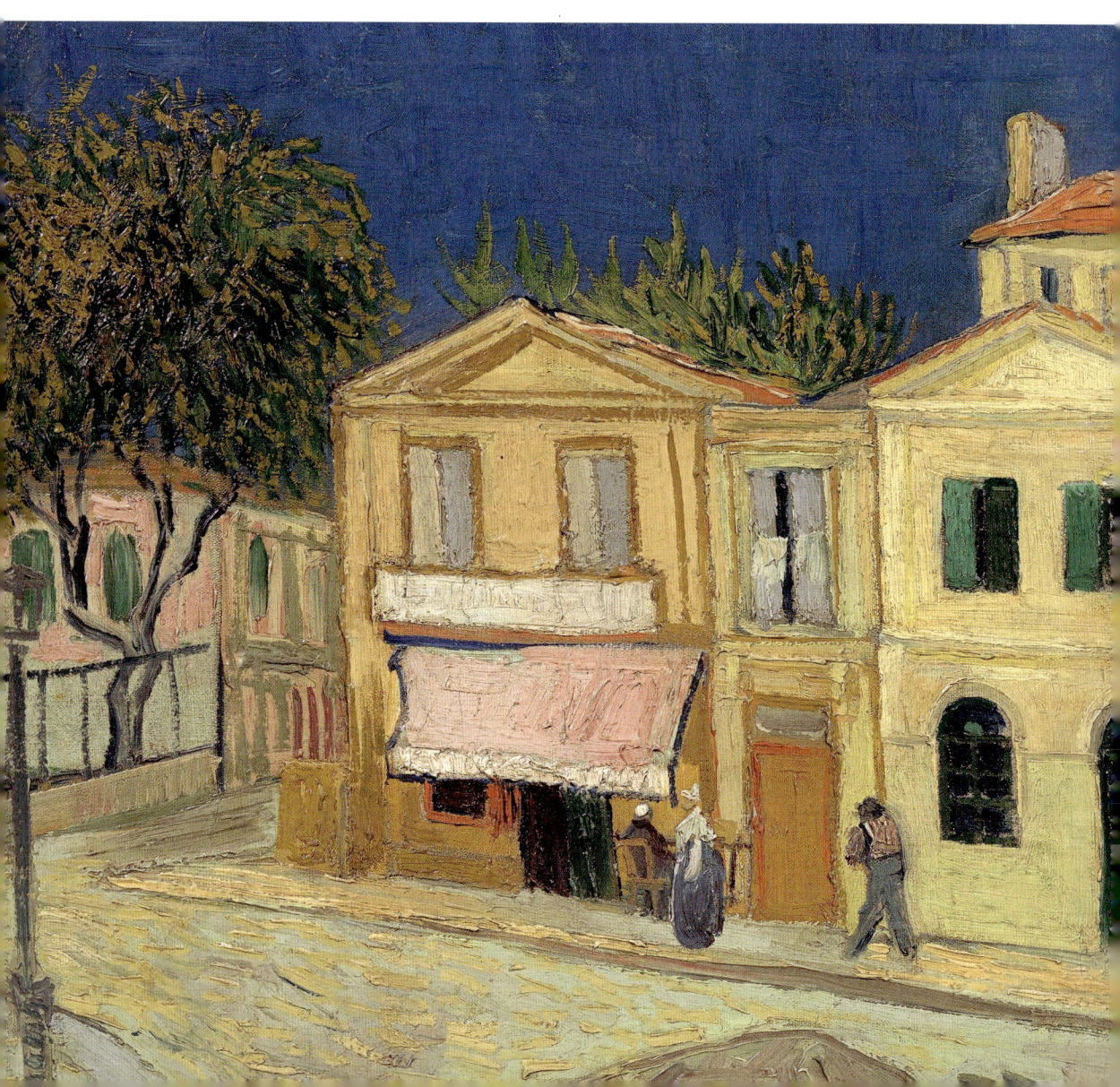

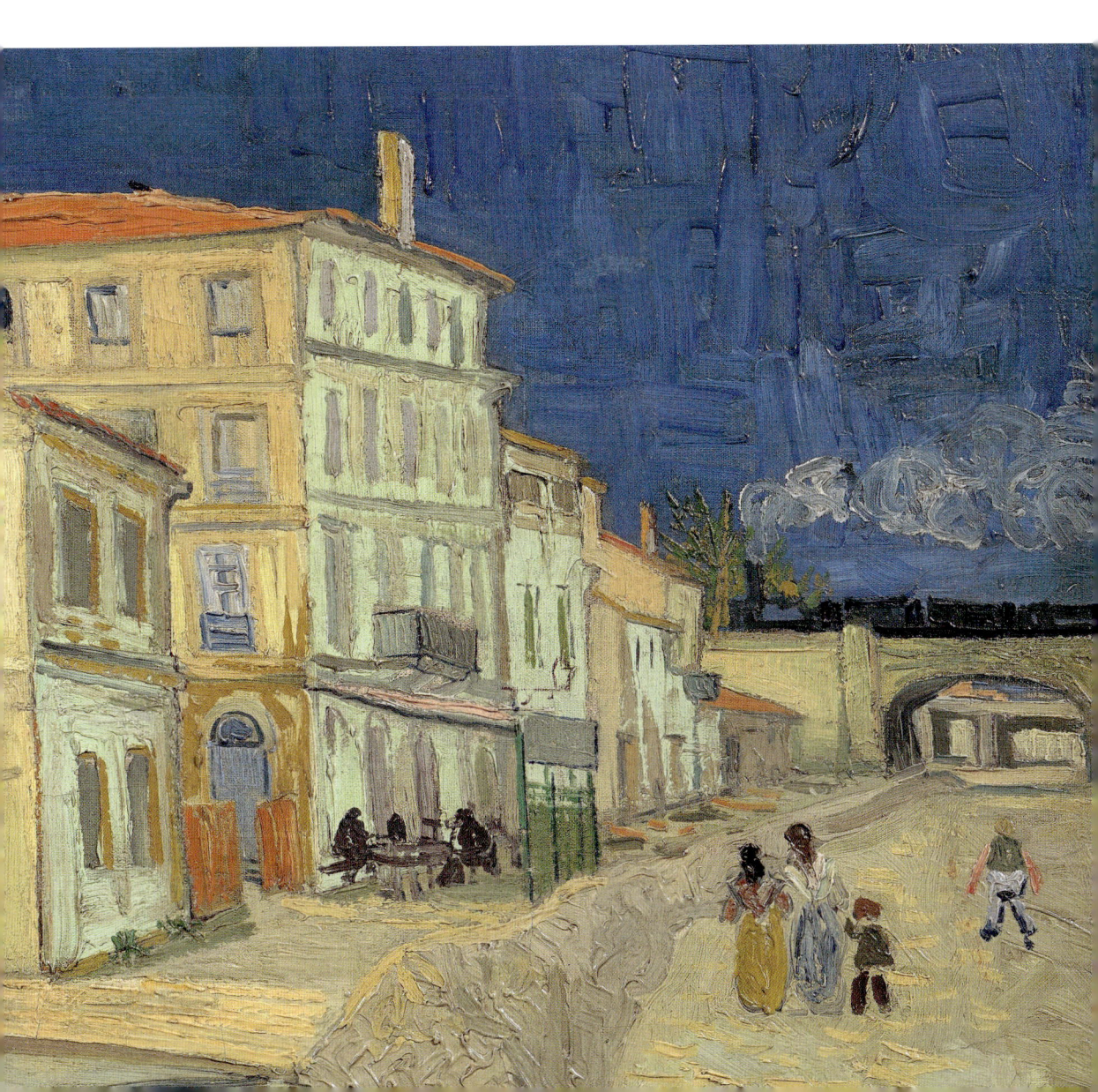

Vincent Willem van Gogh was born in the Dutch village of Zundert on 30 March 1853. His parents were Anna and Theodorus van Gogh, his father a vicar in the small town near Breda. Vincent's birth was followed by five others, those of his sisters Lies, Anna and Wil and his brothers Theo and Cor.

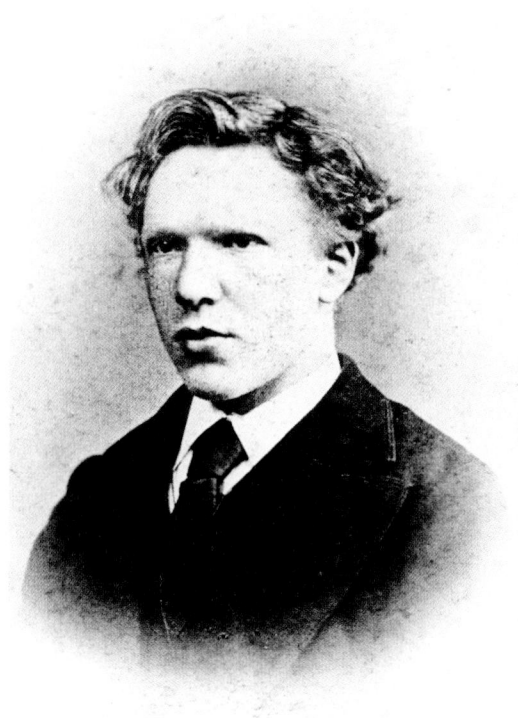

Vincent at the age of 19, 1873

Vincent first attended the local village school, later a boarding school nearby. In 1866 he proceeded to middle school in neighbouring Tilburg, where drawing was part of the curriculum. His drawing teacher was the painter Constantin Huysmans, who in his pictures devoted himself primarily to landscapes and peasant interiors. But Vincent's schooling ended in the middle of the school year, in March 1868; the reason is unclear. At that point his uncle Cent, who was a partner in an art shop in The Hague, took him in. Cent also arranged for employment for his nephew—the young Vincent began an apprenticeship in the local branch of the French art dealer Goupil & Cie. During his training Vincent became increasingly interested in art and began to draw. And as he became familiar with prints, paintings and drawings from various stylistic movements he began collecting himself. He started a woodcut collection, one to which he constantly added with purchases and trades with Theo and with friends. Vincent wrote his first letters to his brother during this period in The Hague. Theo—actually Theodorus — was four years younger and would become Vincent's most important support.

When he was twenty Vincent was transferred to the gallery's London branch. He was enthusiastic about his work, eager to become familiar with English painters and looked forward to learning English. In fact the Dutch speaker soon became fluent in both English and French as well as his mother tongue and would later even switch from one to the other in his letters. While Vincent was off in London, his brother Theo began his

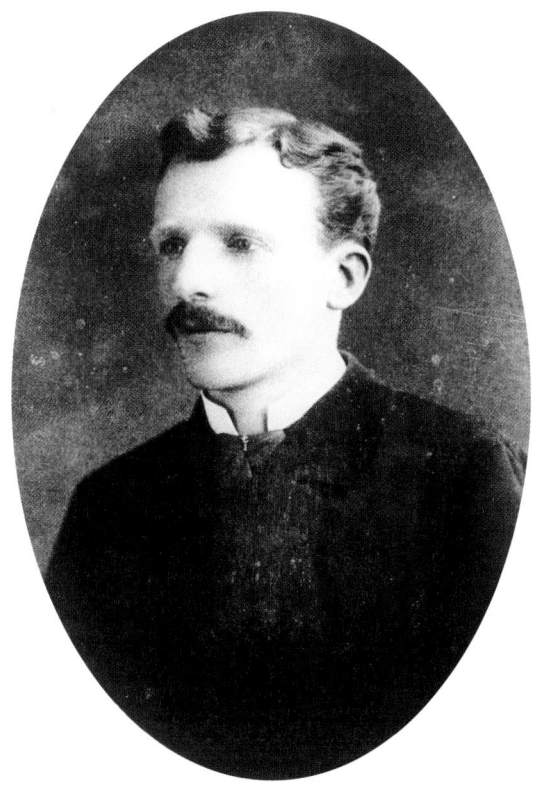

Theo van Gogh, c. 1888

Vincent readily familiarised himself with London's art scene. Popular English art with its working-class themes appealed to him and he collected and continued drawing himself. But his work in the art dealership was unrewarding. He had unhappily fallen in love with his landlady's daughter and this unrequited love did not exactly foster a desire to work. In May 1875 Vincent was finally transferred to Paris, where he worked for Goupil barely another year and with little enthusiasm. His ambitions as an art dealer subsided; he now gave his full attention to Bible study. Even while in London he had become interested in the idea of preaching and when he was dismissed in March 1876, he took it up again. Instead of going home he chose to go back to England. There he worked at a small school as a supply teacher and pursued his desire to take up preaching. At Christmastime he returned to Holland, planning to stay only through the holidays. At his parents' behest he did not return to England, however, but stayed close by. For a few months he worked in a bookshop, in a job his family had arranged for him. But soon his Bible study consumed him; he determined to study theology and follow in his father's footsteps. He wanted to become a pastor—a "sower of the Word", as he put it in a letter.

In May 1877 Vincent therefore moved to his uncle's in Amsterdam, where he prepared for admission to the university, mainly by studying Greek and Latin. At this time his brother Theo helped him by sending small parcels, sometimes stamps, sometimes the tobacco he could not do

own apprenticeship, likewise as an art dealer, in Goupil's Brussels branch. The two brothers began a regular correspondence. Most of Vincent's letters to Theo are preserved, providing us with glimpses into his life and work.

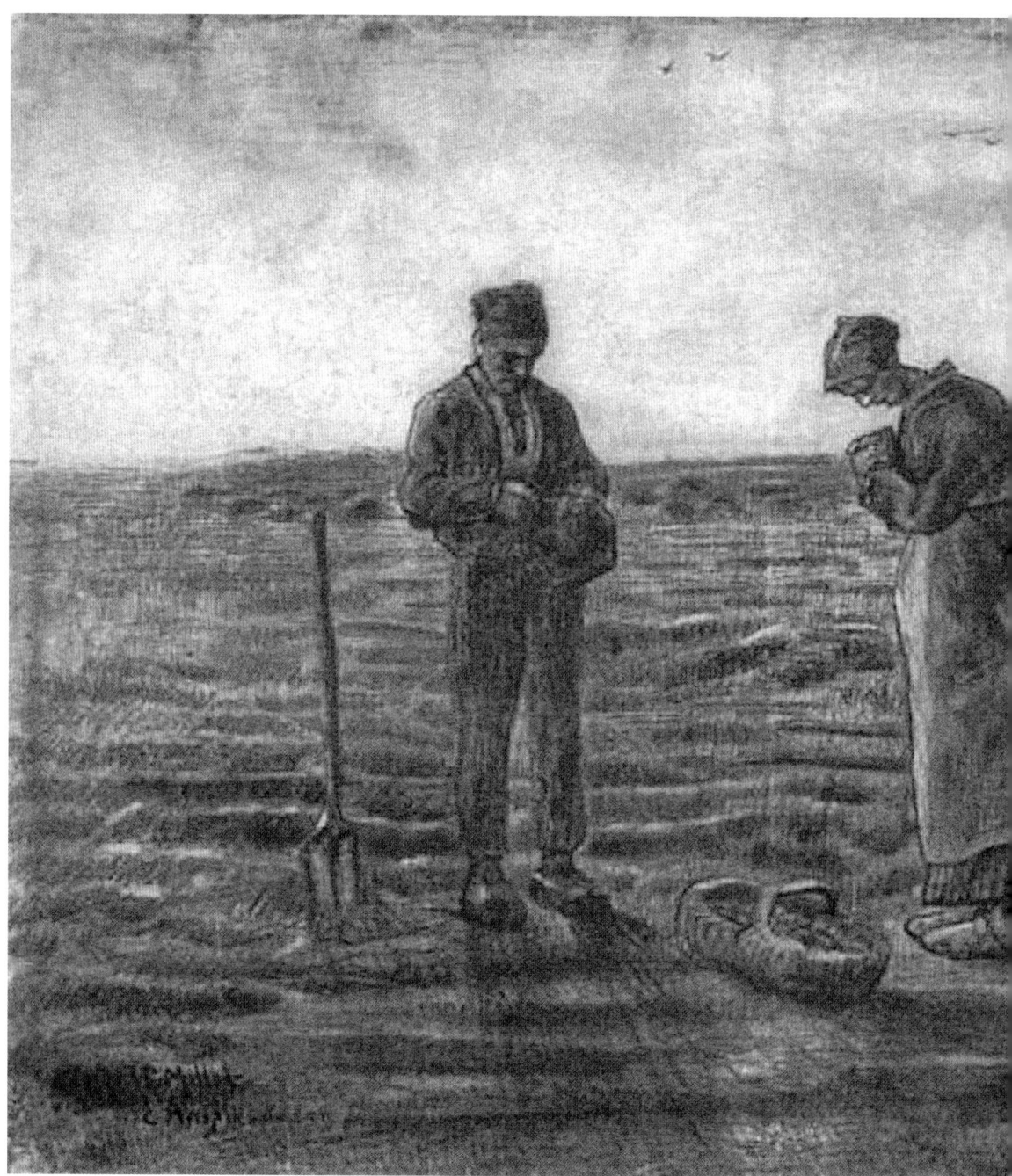

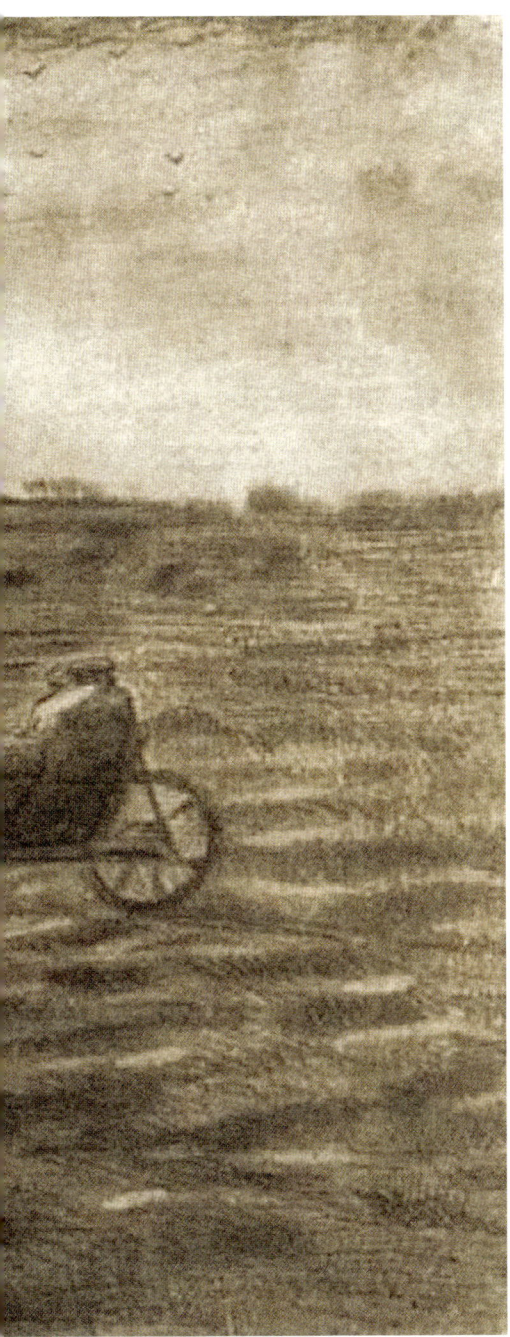

L'Angélus du soir (after Millet), 1880

without. After a little more than a year, however, in August 1878, Vincent gave up his study plans in order to reach his true goal still faster: by becoming a missionary.

In Laeken, near Brussels, the twenty-five-year-old enrolled in a training course for missionaries, but soon dropped out. In November he moved to the Borinage, a coal-mining area in the south of Belgium. There he worked as a missionary, organised Bible studies and tended to the sick. In the process he gradually gave away everything he owned. His identification with the impoverished region's miners to the point of selflessness left him unstable. For that reason, though he worked for the church for a few months as a lay preacher, his appointment was not extended. Nevertheless, frequently going for weeks without a cent to live on, Vincent stayed in the Borinage for nearly two years.

At this time his contact with Theo was only sporadic; he distanced himself from his family. In the desolate mining region he found himself at a low point, yet his family's urging, finally conveyed to him by Theo, only occasioned an even longer silence between the two brothers. In spite of everything, Vincent retained a lively interest in art and literature. Shortly after his arrival in the Borinage he began making drawings of his surroundings. In the few letters he did write to Theo in these years he reported how much he was taken with the "strange, remarkable and picturesque region".

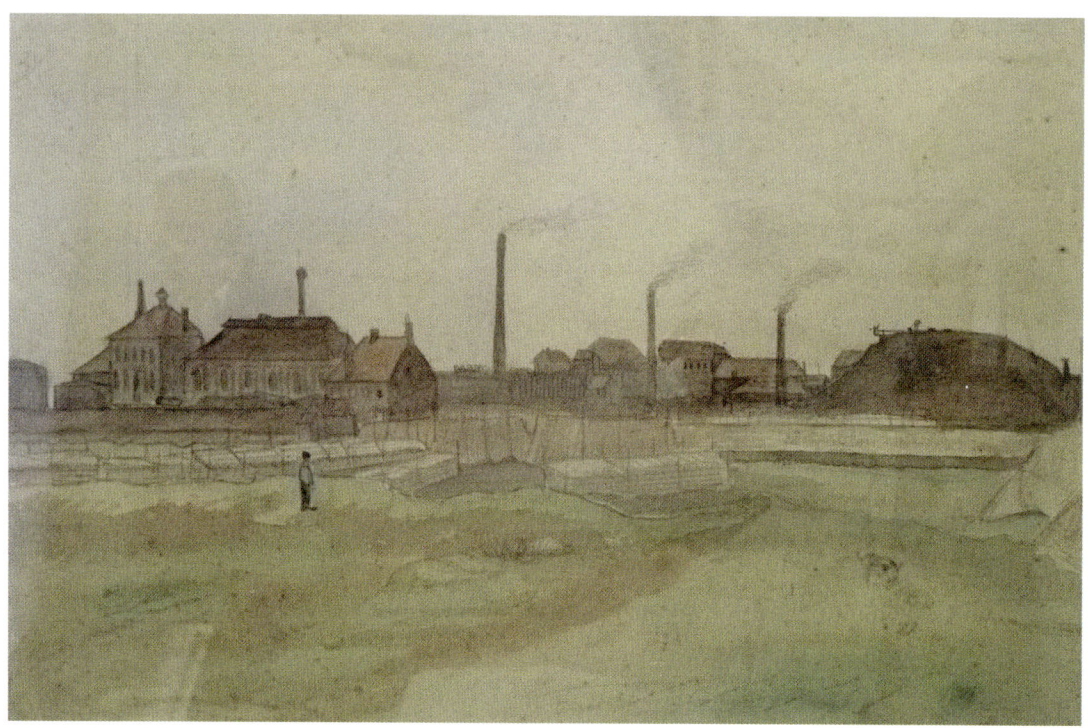

Coking Factory in the Borinage, 1879

First Steps as a Draughtsman and Painter

Thanks to his drawing, things finally started to look up for him. After a long period of self-doubt he began to feel that his life was back on track. Having spent long months working on his own, drawing after works of art he found in books and sketching the miners and the desolate surrounding landscape, he informed his younger brother of his new career choice: he wanted to become an artist.

Once the twenty-seven-year-old had made this decision the relationship between the two brothers changed. "But now I'm going full speed ahead—painting has to be furthered with all the strength we can apply to it." The 'we' included Theo; the plural found its way into his letters once he had set out on an artistic path. And Theo's collaboration was indeed substantial. He provided money for rent and food and sent canvas, paints, paper and brushes from Paris. But his financial support was the least of it; as is clear from Vincent's many letters, Theo gave his brother much more: "But write, my boy, even if you haven't any money, for I need your kindness, it is no less a help to me than the money." For long years Theo was the only confidant Vincent admitted, the one to whom he granted insight

Letter from Vincent to Theo van Gogh (recto), 29 December 1881

into his creative process and his personal life in endless rambling letters.

Even when he began to draw in earnest it was clear to van Gogh that he needed to have art and artists around him, that simply copying out of printed sources was not enough. Again he repeatedly considered enrolling in an art academy: "There are laws of proportion, light and shadow and perspective that one has to know in order to be able to draw something." So in the autumn of 1880 he moved to Brussels hoping to find likeminded people there and for a few months he attended courses at the Brussels Academy, where he became acquainted with the painter Anton

van Rappard, with whom a years-long friendship developed. But the Academy's instruction failed to satisfy him. After six months in Brussels he moved on, discouraged about his progress. In May 1881 he moved to his parents' house, now in Etten. There he continued to work on the basics of drawing on his own, experimenting with various drawing materials and dealing with such technical problems as perspective, proportions and light and shadow. He kept his brother informed about his progress, often in great detail, telling him about the new techniques he was working on.

He was pleased that Theo had found his footing after his apprenticeship in the art business.

Woman ('Sien') Seated near the Stove, 1882

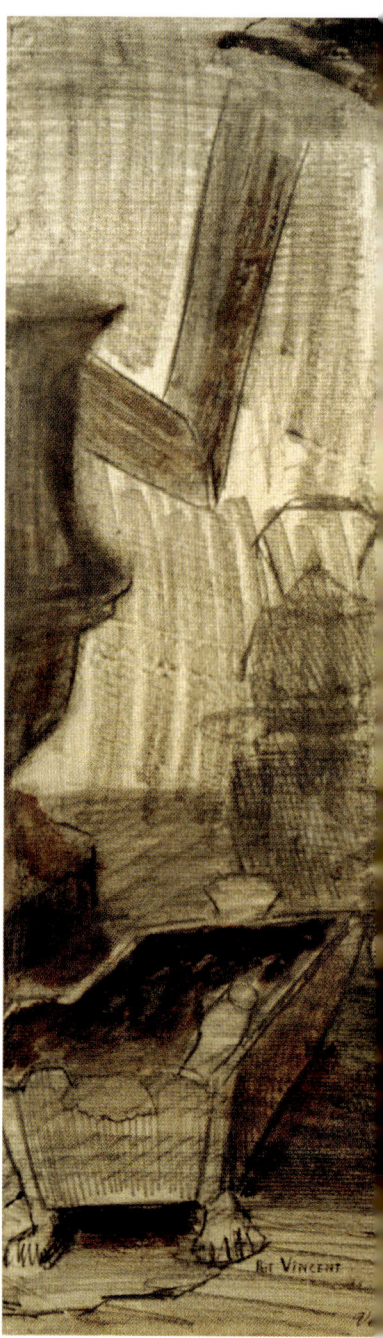

In countless letters the brothers discussed their shared passion for art. Theo was now working in the Goupil firm's Paris headquarters. From the period's undisputed art capital he supplied his brother with works to emulate, whether sheets from his own collection or pages-long descriptions of works he was encountering as a young art dealer.

The turn of the years 1881/82 found Vincent settled in The Hague, a centre of Dutch art life, where he continued his artistic training. He attended classes in life drawing, practising the rendering of figures, and for a brief time Anton Mauve, a leading member of The Hague's painting school and a cousin of his by marriage, instructed him. In evening drawing classes Mauve would critique Vincent's work and give him valuable pointers. Most importantly, Mauve gave Vincent a box of pigments and encouraged him to turn to painting. After two years of drawing exclusively van Gogh began to paint.

In the spring he met the former seamstress and prostitute Clasina Maria Hoornik and moved with her and her daughter into an atelier apartment. His family promptly distanced itself from him; even Theo expressed incomprehension in view of this liaison with Sien, as Vincent called her. In the next months he produced several drawings of the small family and in the summer, when Sien gave birth to a son, he immediately drew him as well.

Meanwhile Vincent was discovering colours and beginning to paint outdoors. By the autumn he was ready to try painting in oils. Theo had previously visited him and promised to supply him

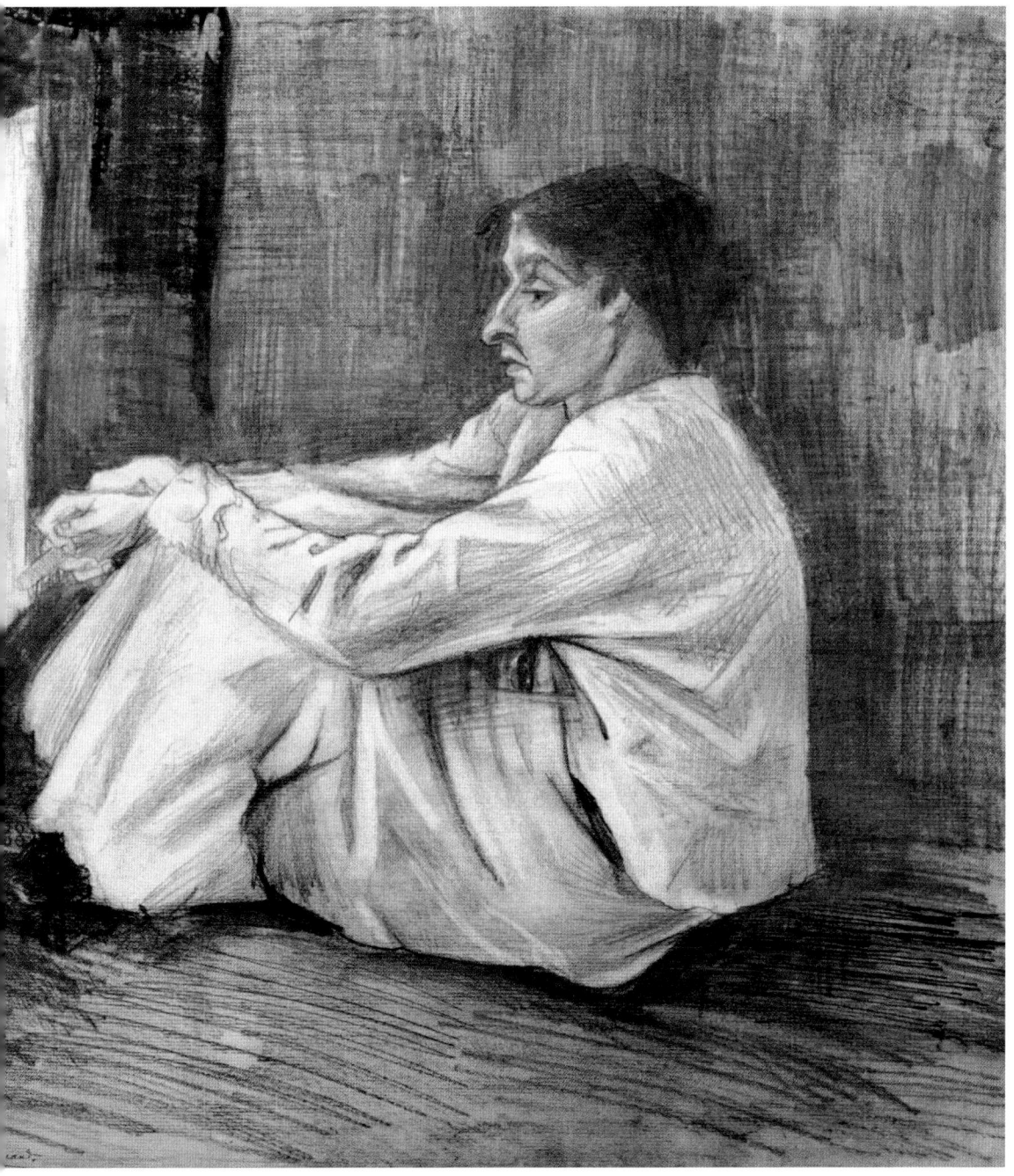

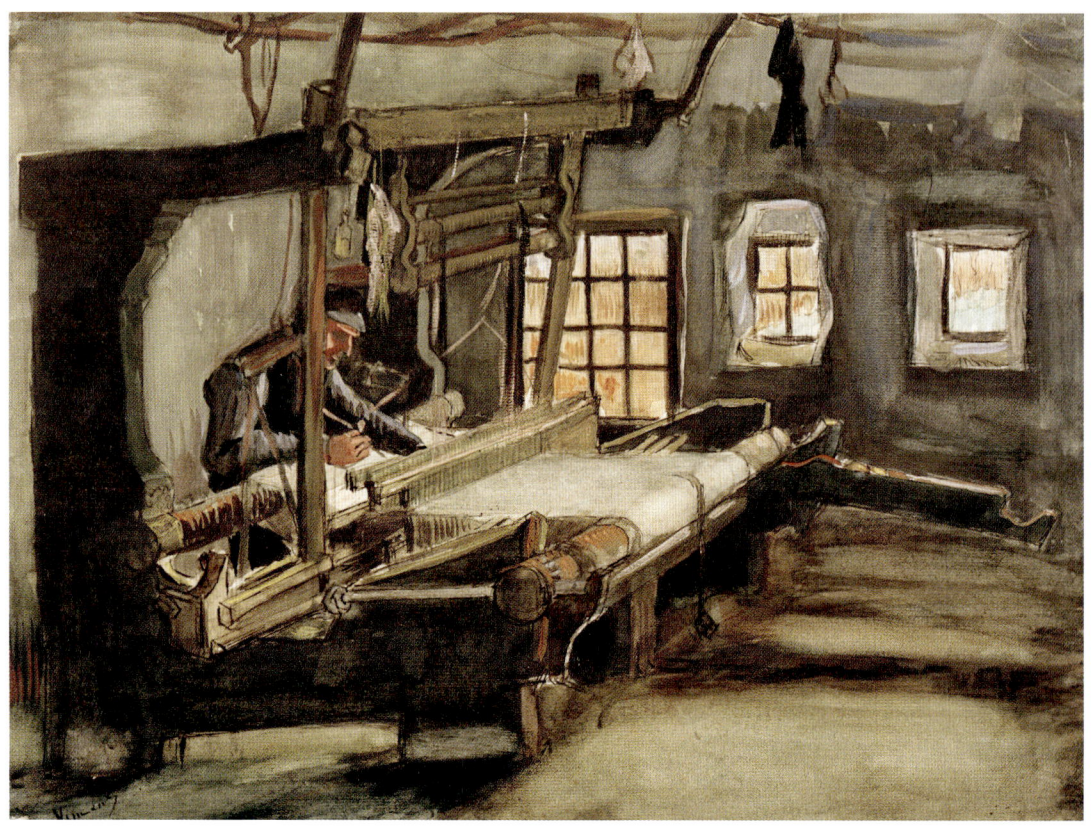

Weaver, 1883/84

with painting materials—also financial support for another year. Vincent excitedly began to shower him with letters: "You mustn't resent the fact that I am already writing again—it is only to tell you that I am getting particularly great pleasure out of painting." He even started referring to himself as a painter and from now on nothing would stop him. His subjects were labourers, in the fields, in a poor part of town, while rag picking. He painted outdoors, even in the rain, barely taking time to eat and drink and considered painting a cure for his insomnia. His health had meanwhile deteriorated to the point that he was forced to spend several weeks in a hospital. Despite the difficult circumstances, he made great progress artistically, but still felt far from his goal.

In October 1883 he separated from Sien and her children. His money worries had become acute and he was threatened with garnishment. Theo ultimately stepped in and paid his brother's debts. Vincent now moved to Drenthe in Holland's rural north, but after three months he turned his back on that lonely landscape of moorland and heath and took refuge with his parents, then living in Nuenen, near Eindhoven, a second time. He set up a small atelier there.

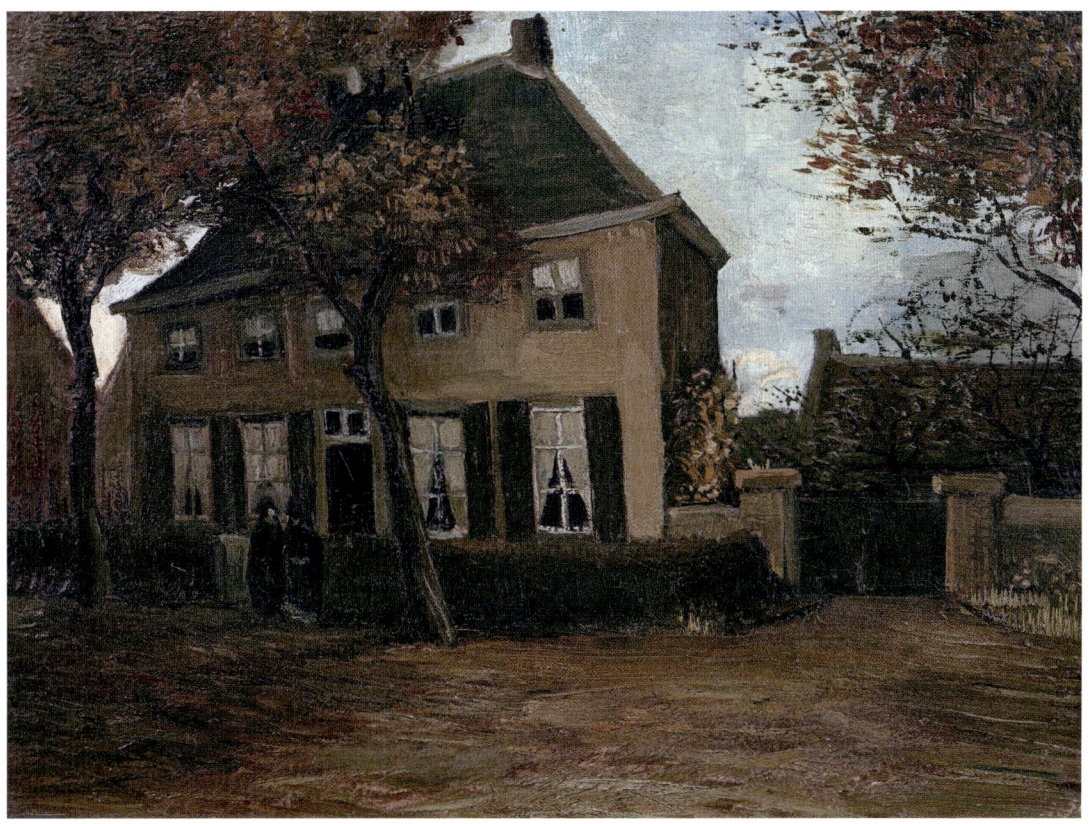

The Vicarage at Nuenen, 1885

In the early summer of 1884 the two brothers came to a new understanding. Vincent wanted to consider Theo's financial support as payment for his works. Up to the end he maintained that his entire oeuvre was Theo's achievement, "for the money from you, that you supply me with, costs effort enough, as I know, gives you the right to consider half of whatever good comes from my work your own creation". From this point on he sent his brother all his studies, pictures and drawings—he wanted to feel he was earning his pay. In return Theo sent him not only cash, pigments and canvas, but also detailed reports about new art movements, artists and techniques, exhibitions and dealers. In the summer, when Theo paid visits in Nuenen, the brothers also discussed the painting of the Impressionists, which was causing a sensation back in Paris. Vincent was meanwhile painting and drawing the weavers, peasants and labourers in his north Brabant homeland. The region was a centre of Dutch textile production and in Nuenen, despite industrialisation, weaving was still done by hand. Van Gogh had trouble picturing weavers and looms, desperate to show them in the proper perspective. When no models were available he again painted still lifes: baskets

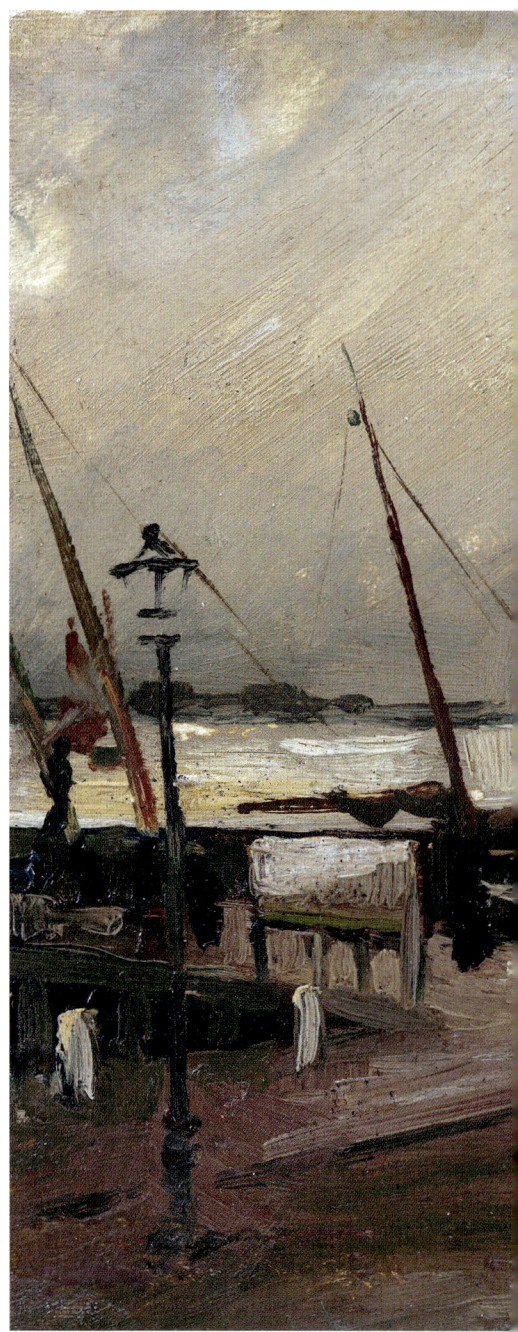

of apples or potatoes, birds' nests, the peasants' heavy clogs, ceramic jars—everything in dark, earthy colours. Between December 1883 and November 1885 he produced roughly 500 works, paintings, watercolours, drawings and studies. In Nuenen he felt he was in the ideal setting: "Moreover there's nothing I require beyond sitting deep in the countryside among the peasants and painting peasant life."

For months he prepared for his first large oil painting, *The Potato Eaters* (page 48), with countless preliminary studies. In it he pictured a peasant family around the dinner table. Since the end of 1884 he had made more than forty drawings and paintings of its five figures' heads and hands—all in advance of a painting that would become the masterpiece of his Netherlandish years. But before Vincent began to paint he urged Theo to show sketches of it around in Paris, hoping to call its attention to potential buyers. He also had a lithograph of the picture printed, but neither Theo nor the contacted art dealers were impressed. In May Vincent sent the finished work to his brother, but Theo and his artist friends remained critical.

Van Gogh again delved into the pictures of old masters. On a visit to Amsterdam those of Rembrandt and Frans Hals impressed him most of all. He was again drawn to city life and in November 1885 the thirty-two-year-old left for Antwerp, where for three months he studied at the Academy. He hoped that urban surroundings would bring him new artist contacts and portrait

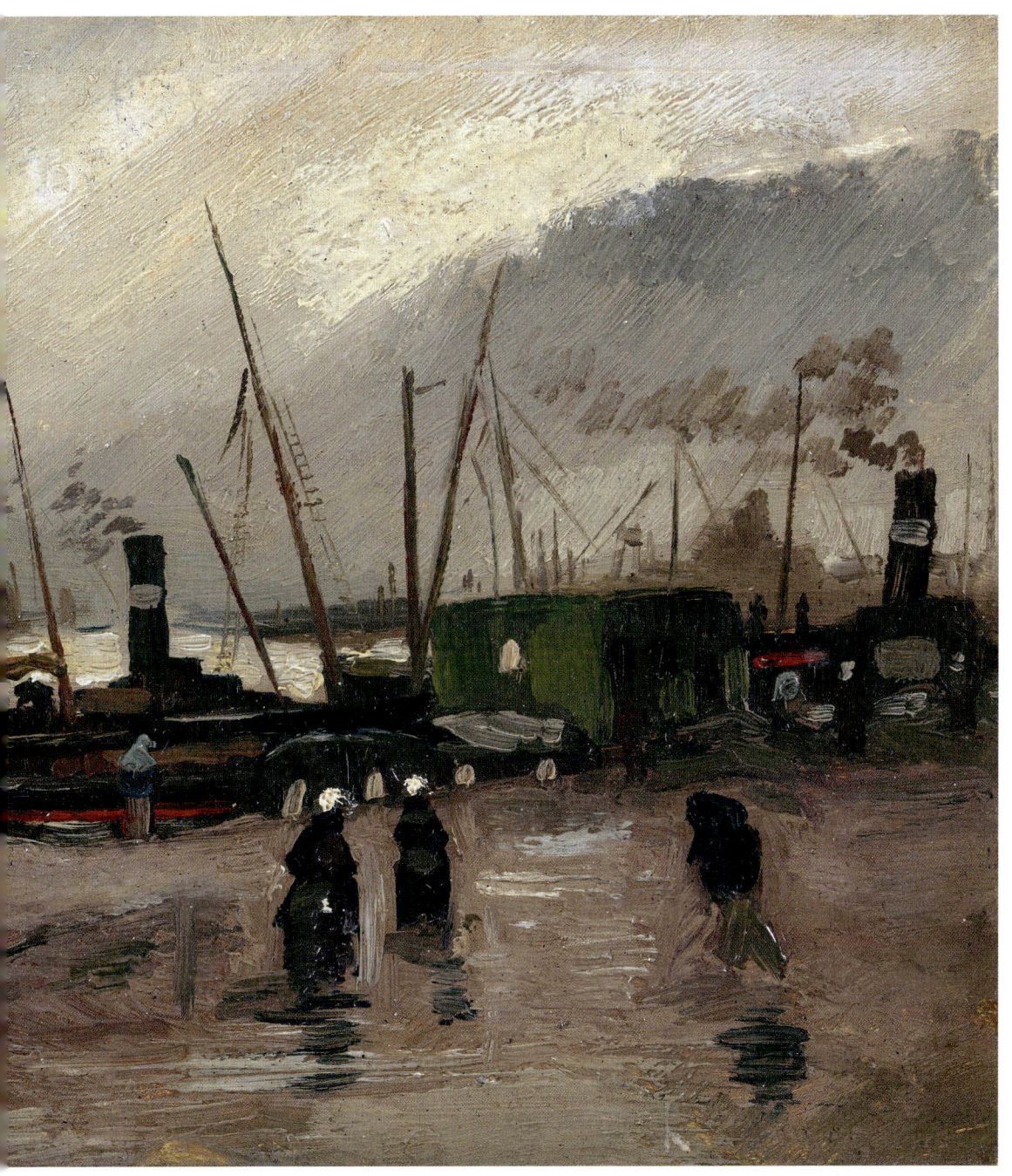

commissions. As he wrote to his brother, his choice was ultimately between an atelier without work in Nuenen and work without an atelier in Antwerp. He opted for the latter and immediately got into contact with art galleries there, at one of which he was able to exhibit some of his works. Antwerp's museums inspired him; he discovered Japanese woodcuts there and decorated the walls of his workroom with the colourful prints.

But the hoped-for success failed to materialise. Once again his debts piled up and his health was rapidly declining. Even as a young man he had complained of insomnia, headaches and toothaches, a recalcitrant stomach, nervousness, being frequently 'in turmoil', anxiousness and nightmares. He wrote to Theo at length about his routine, which included little rest. We can conclude from his stacks of letters and hundreds of paintings and drawings that he was working at a feverish rate. He frequently neglected to eat, even when he had the money he preferred to hire models in order to practise figure painting. In Antwerp the state of his health became truly critical for the first time; his teeth were close to falling out and he would deaden his hunger pangs by smoking. Yet he hit upon a new plan: he would join his brother in Paris. At least in the art metropolis he would find new inspiration and come into contact with other painters.

Among Artists: Van Gogh in Montmartre

In March 1886 van Gogh abruptly headed for Paris, where Theo took him in. In June the two moved into a large apartment in Montmartre's rue Lepic. At this time the quarter in the north of the city was still rural, known for its windmills and gardens, and any number of artists lived and worked there. Vincent threw himself into the city's art scene, then dominated by Impressionism. He visited the eighth and last Impressionist exhibition shortly after his arrival. He later wrote to his friend, the painter Horace Mann Livens: "In Antwerp I didn't even know who the Impressionists were, now I have seen them and although I am not a member of the club, I still admired some of the Impressionists' pictures." Little by little van Gogh familiarised himself with the Impressionists' motifs, their light palette and their sketch-like style of painting.

In his first months in Paris Vincent painted his nearby surroundings: from the apartment window he could look down onto rue Lepic and the roofs of neighbouring buildings, which he painted again and again. He also produced a whole series of flower paintings; in these still lifes featuring large bouquets of lilies, roses or poppies he ventured a new way of painting with stronger colours. They let him experiment with shapes and colours without a great deal of trouble. As he wrote to his sister Wil—actually Willemien—he painted these pictures as colour studies, that he wanted to get used to tonal values different from the dark, earthy ones he had formerly relied on. Van Gogh

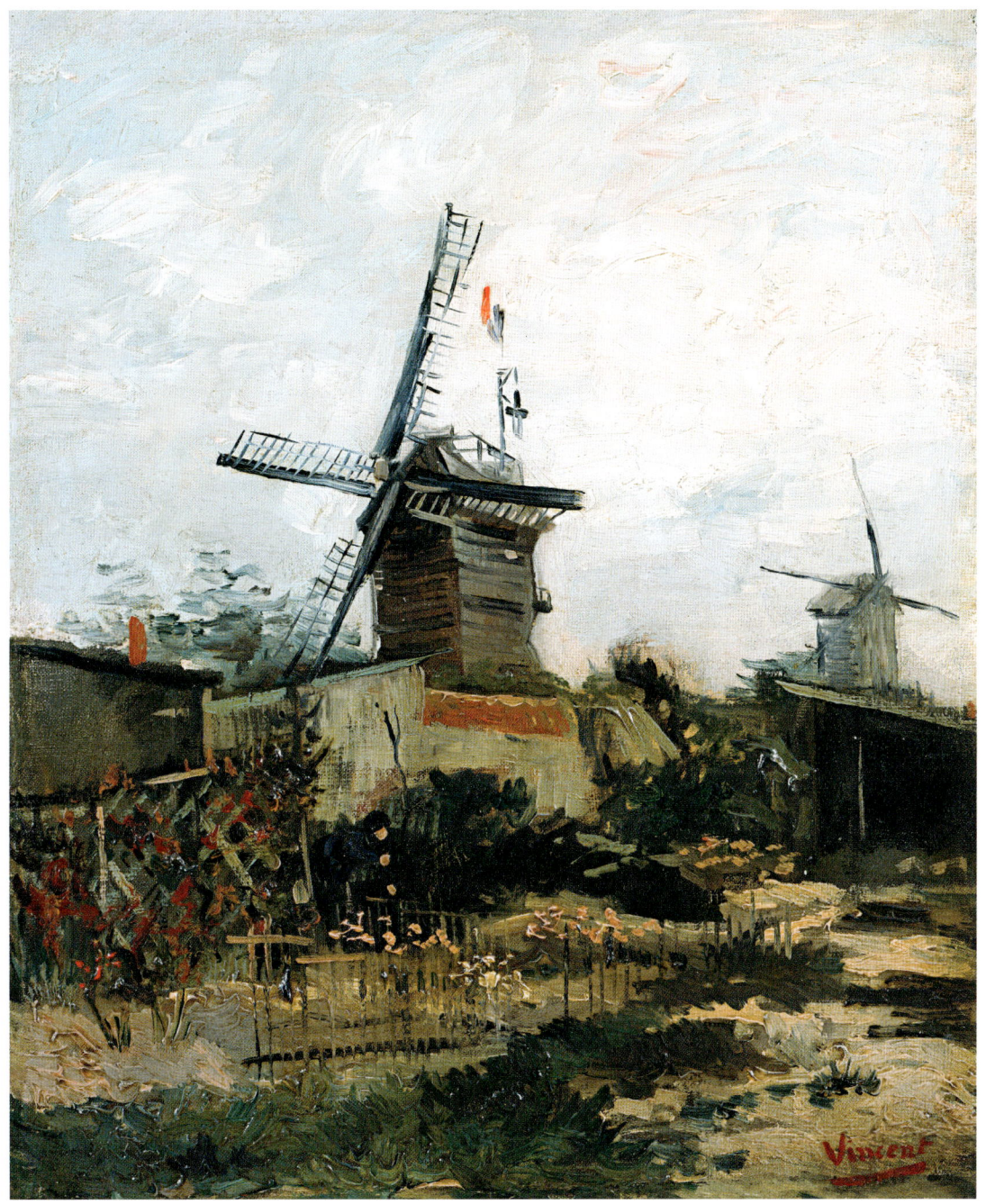

made tremendous progress in these months. His palette gradually lightened and he began to place the new colours on his canvas with short, often visible brush strokes.

After his arrival he worked for a few months in the atelier of the history painter Fernand Cormon on the nearby Boulevard de Clichy. There Cormon maintained an open studio where artists could draw from sculptures or models and in which he occasionally taught. It gave Vincent an opportunity to talk to many other painters: Henri de Toulouse-Lautrec, Émile Bernard and Louis Anquetin were regular visitors. Van Gogh traded works with them, found friends and likeminded souls and thus immersed himself in the artists' scene around Montmartre. Near the van Gogh brothers' apartment was Julien Tanguy's shop selling painting supplies, which Vincent frequented and which was another artists' meeting place. Tanguy not only sold them materials, he also repeatedly displayed and sold their works in his shop. Van Gogh's paintings soon appeared in his show window as well. Best of all, the Dutchman was introduced to many fellow painters and their works at Tanguy's. Along with the Impressionists, the paint dealer particularly admired the works of the Pointillists. Among them was the painter Paul Signac, who van Gogh came to know and with whom he frequently painted in the spring of 1887. The two would head out into the city's northern suburbs and paint the Seine landscape in Clichy, Asnières and Saint-Ouen.

Theo van Gogh had meanwhile become the director of the Goupil firm's Montmartre branch. He had first shown pictures by Impressionist artists in the spring of 1886 and was acquainted with many of them. He was therefore able to forge contacts between them and his brother. One was Camille Pissarro, who had joined the Impressionists and who—like Vincent—was inspired by country life. Vincent, in turn, was able to repay Theo, the art dealer, by introducing his new painter friends to him. Vincent had, for example, recently become acquainted with the painter Paul Gauguin and soon Theo became his gallerist. The Japanese colour prints that van Gogh had come to admire while in Antwerp were then the rage in Paris. Since the middle of the century these so-called *crêpes* had found their way to Europe, initially as packing paper for Asian wares. The colourful prints owed their name to the crinkled, crepe-like paper used for them. They frequently employed unusual perspectives, radical views from above or below, for example, and motifs cut off by the picture edges—features now being seen in works by contemporary European artists. In spite of his small budget, Vincent became a major collector of them. The brothers' Montmartre apartment was soon decorated with *crêpes* and Vincent's fascination with them influenced his own painting. He briefly even considered dealing in such prints himself. He organised an exhibition of them in the Café Le Tambourin, a Montmartre restaurant he often patronised. He also showed flower paintings from his first summer in Paris there and even had a brief affair with the café's owner, the former artists' model Agostina Segatori. This was not the only exhibition venue he made use of; he also

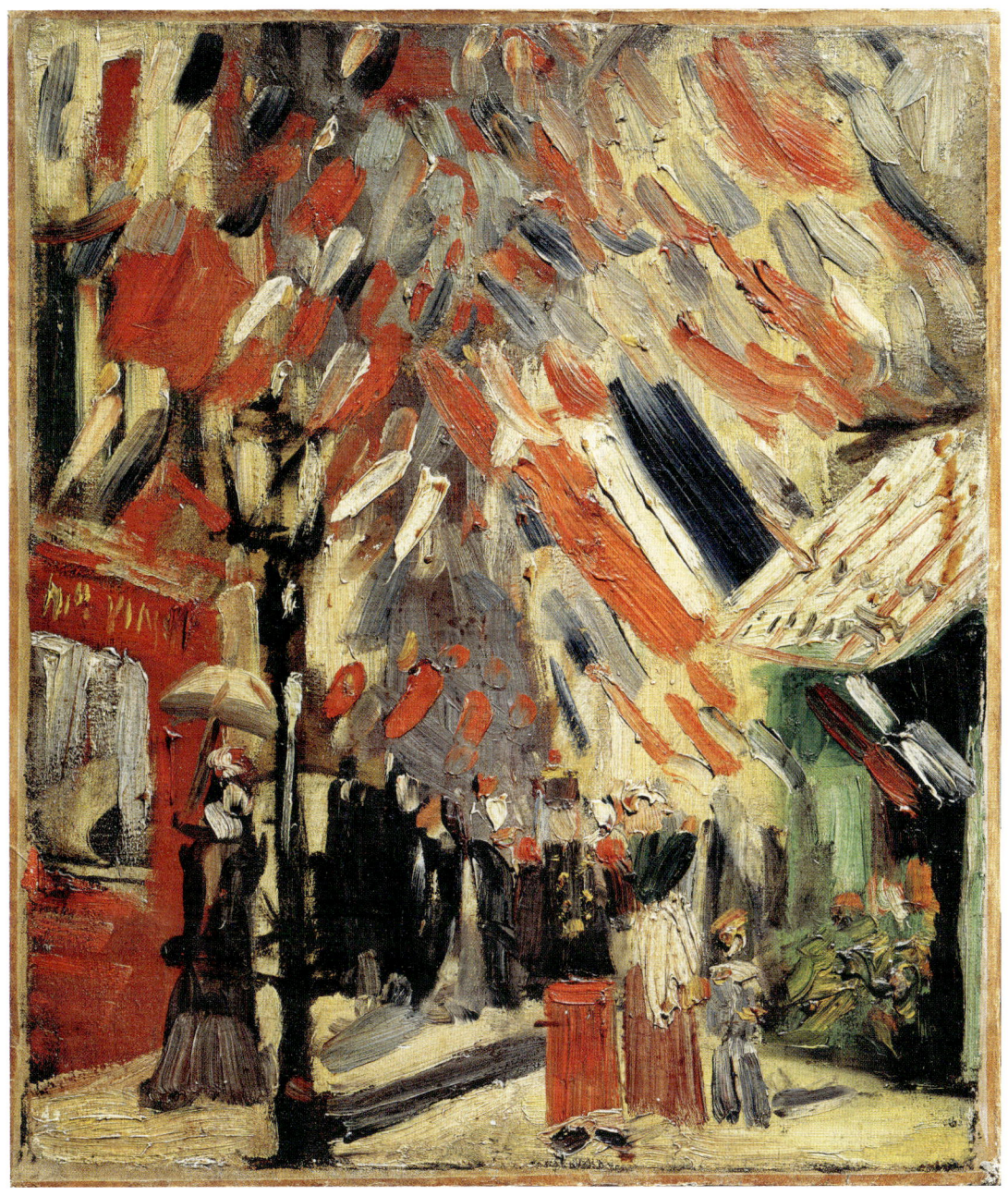

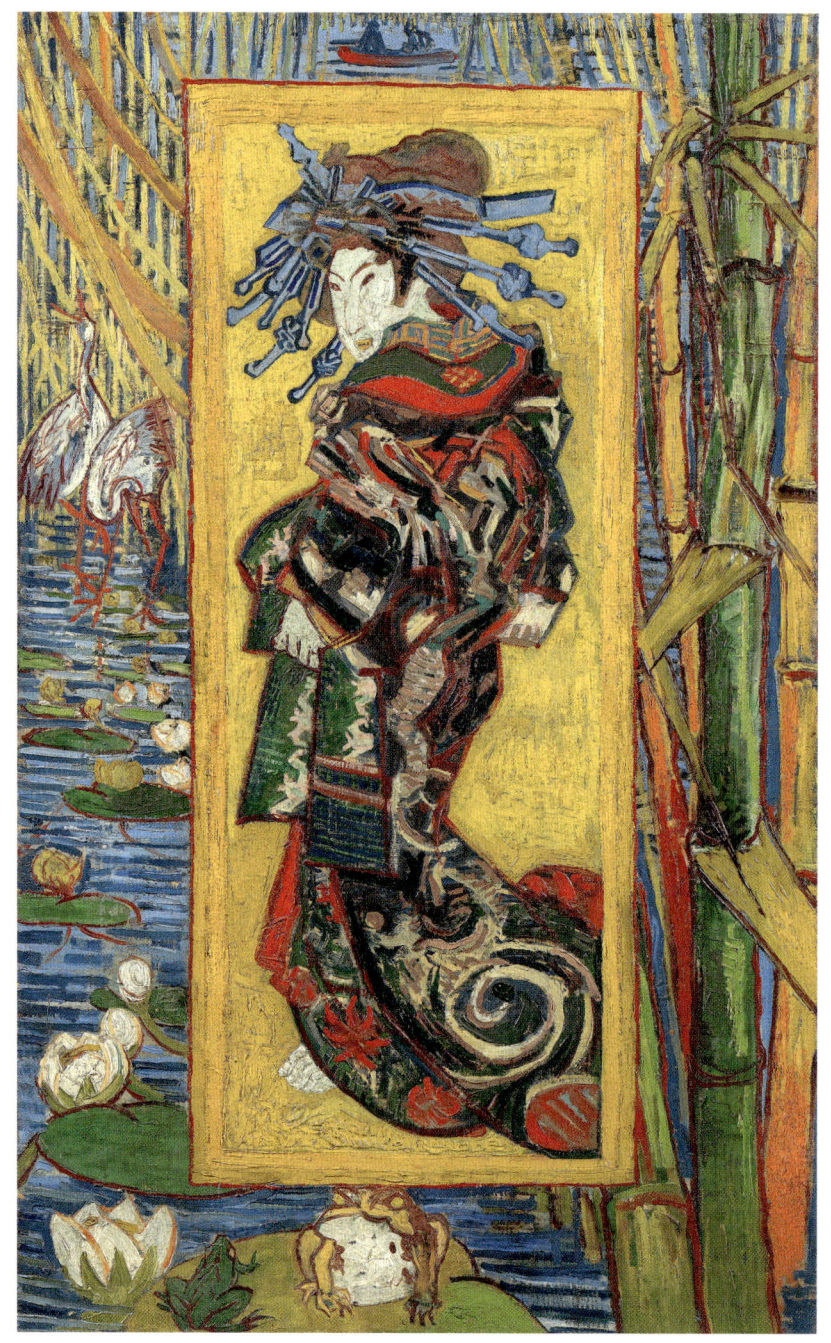

Courtesan (after Kesai Eisen), 1887

organised two other shows of his own works and those of his artist friends. For one in the popular Restaurant du Châlet, also nearby, van Gogh put together 100 works, roughly half of them painted by himself. He failed to sell anything of his own there, but he did trade two of his pictures for one by Paul Gauguin that he treasured.

During the two years that van Gogh spent in Paris he radically changed the way he painted and developed a highly personal style. Living for the first time in an artistically charged environment, he became fully familiar with the newest trends in painting at his typical fast rate and, in his own work, experimented with a number of the stylistic devices being used by Paris's Impressionist and Pointillist artists. He meanwhile studied Japanese woodcuts as intensively as the art of old masters in the capital's many museums. Along with his painting style van Gogh also changed his palette, leaving behind the earthy tones and strong shadows of the past and turning to bold colours and sharp contrasts instead.

In these two Paris years van Gogh painted more than 200 pictures. His friend and artist colleague Émile Bernard later recalled that he had known Vincent to produce three paintings in a single day. His frenzied working speed hardly spared his shaky constitution, especially in combination with the bad wine and absinthe that were no less his constant companions than canvases and tubes of paint, as his friend Signac related. Paris was thus a drain on his health; in his second winter there he referred to himself as a "near alcoholic". In February he left Paris, convinced that

elsewhere he would be able to work together with other painters, perhaps even found his own artists' colony. With this dream in his pocket he headed to Provence and the little town of Arles, where he set up his southern atelier. Van Gogh hoped for improvement in the south, not only in his painting but above all in his health. But just like the excessive drinking, the compulsive painting accompanied him to Provence in the spring of 1888 and he charged "at painting like a locomotive".

Painting at Nature's Pace

Provence inspired van Gogh, although it revealed its wintery side on his arrival—there was even snow on the ground. But the intrusion of winter only strengthened his conviction that he was where he belonged. Everything reminded him of the wintry landscapes pictured by Japanese artists and thus Provence wholly conformed to his conception of Japan and he lived there like a Japanese painter in harmony with nature. To Theo, with whom he again regularly corresponded, he complained about the one thing that failed to accord with that image and which upset him in his new home: the mistral. Initially the strong wind even kept him from working outside, but he soon learned to tie sticks to his easel that he could drive into the ground and thus paint in the open in spite of it. As soon as the weather permitted, van Gogh got to work. In the spring he gloried in the fruit blossoms and compulsively captured them on canvas. His orders for pigments from Theo began to accumulate; he needed to hurry, for the bloom wouldn't last long. And the harvest time, which he spent painting in the wheat fields, he found far too brief.

One of the first pieces of news that Vincent received in Provence was a sad one: his former teacher Anton Mauve had died in The Hague. Van Gogh worked with him for only a short time, to be sure, but Mauve's words obviously carried weight. It was he who encouraged Vincent to paint and gave him his first set of pigments. The former teacher's death was a heavy blow. He selected the best of the fruit-blossom canvases he had painted in the past weeks and commissioned Theo to present them to the painter's widow: ". . . in memory of Mauve it strikes me that something light and cheerful is wanted, one needs something delicate and cheerful and nothing weightier than my study".

Almost all of the correspondence between the brothers from these years is preserved, even Theo's letters, so it is easy to follow the dialogue the two maintained. Vincent kept his brother informed about his activities and his ideas for pictures. He painted with incredible speed: in the fifteen months he stayed in Arles he produced nearly 200 paintings, completing one almost every other day. He also made roughly 100 drawings, some of them in large format. The painter found his motifs in and around Arles, mainly in the landscape itself: the area's orchards, flowering meadows, fields and vineyards. But he also produced a few local portraits: he painted his landlady, the gardener and the family of his friend the postman Roulin. In the summer he spent a few days in June on the Mediterranean and even tried his hand at seascapes. From the small fishing village of Saintes-Maries-de-la-Mer he brought back nine drawings and three studies in oils. And soon van Gogh devoted himself to a new motif in several works; he discovered the night sky for his painting and even worked at night, complete with easel, out of doors. In late summer he pictured large bouquets of sunflowers on canvas before being captivated by the autumn grape harvest. In many of his letters he complained that nature did not always cooperate, either the mistral kept him from painting, the summer heat gave him trouble or mosquitoes tortured him while he worked.

Van Gogh found himself in a veritable working fever. He hoped to follow the rhythm of nature with his pictures—and its tempo: "At the moment I'm working on bright yellow plum trees with a thousand black branches. I'm using up an enormous amount of canvas and pigment, but nevertheless hope I am not wasting my money." Working in such a frenzy meant that his need for new painting materials became acute. Always short of money, he constantly worried about replenishing his supply. The pigment orders he placed with Theo in Paris immediately multiplied once he arrived in Arles. It was not unusual for him to squeeze his oil pigments onto the canvas directly out of the tube. His friend Émile Bernard later recalled his extremely costly way of working: his friend did not often use a brush but painted with the tube itself, squeezing out pigment as he worked. Van Gogh gradually

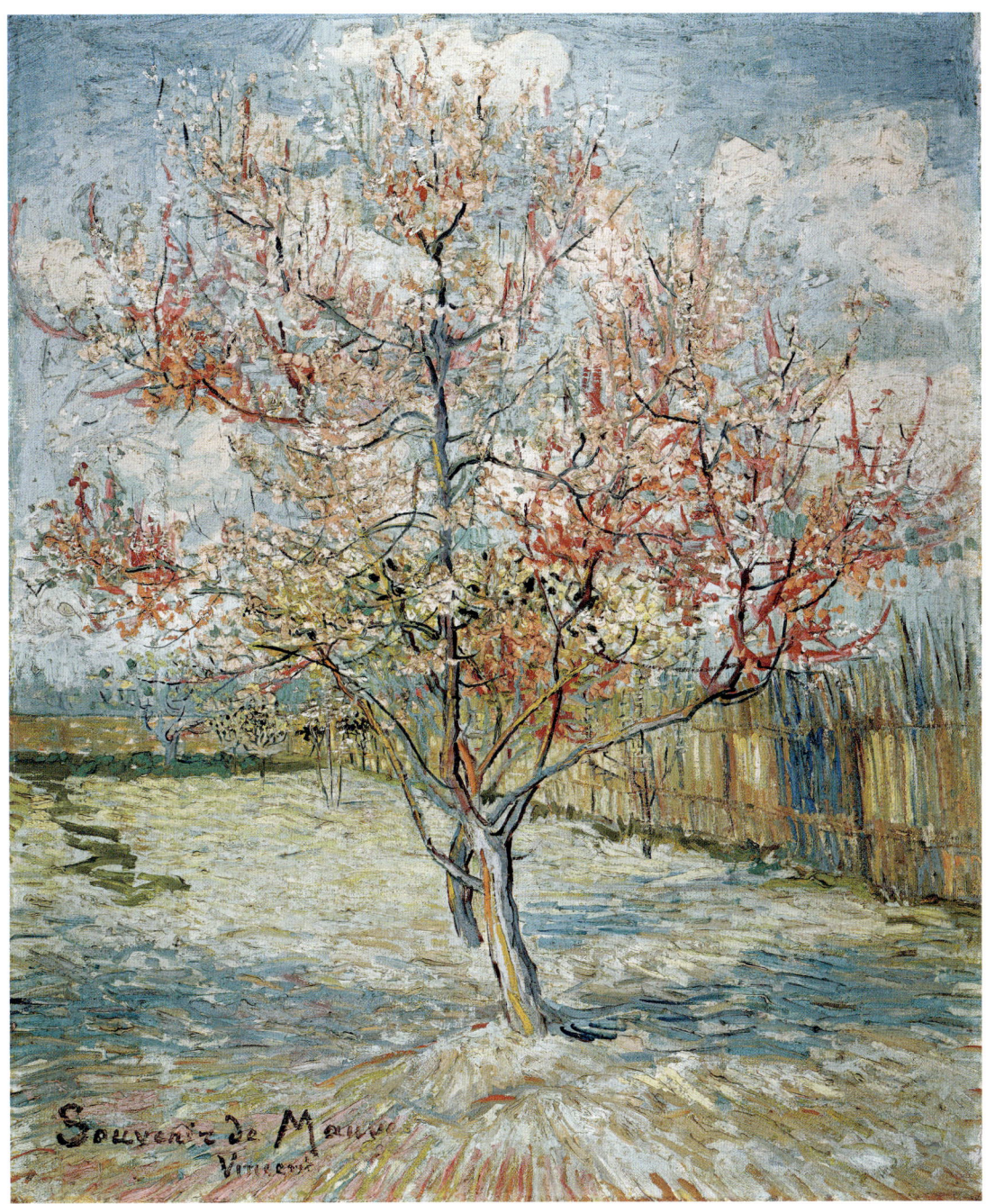

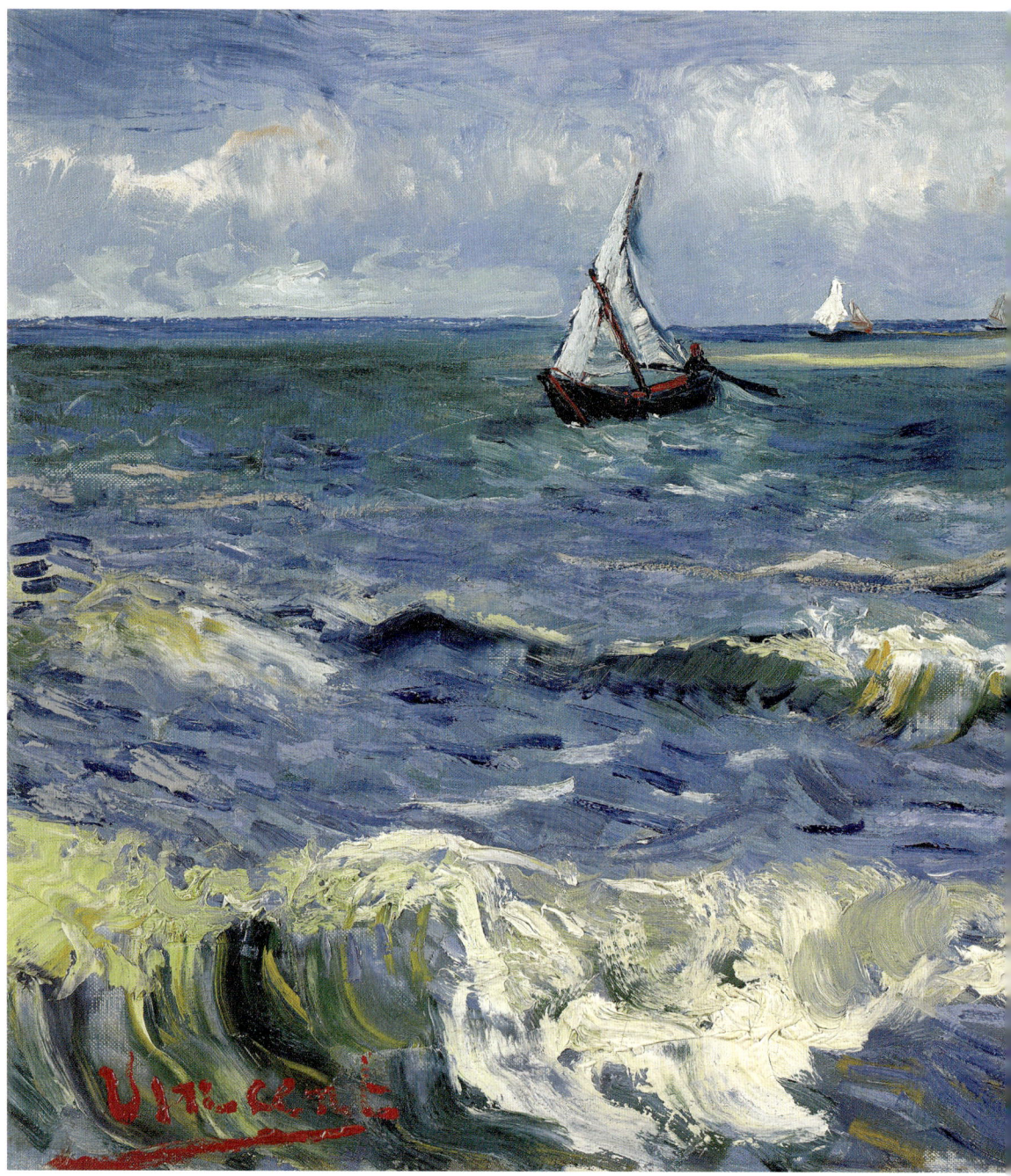

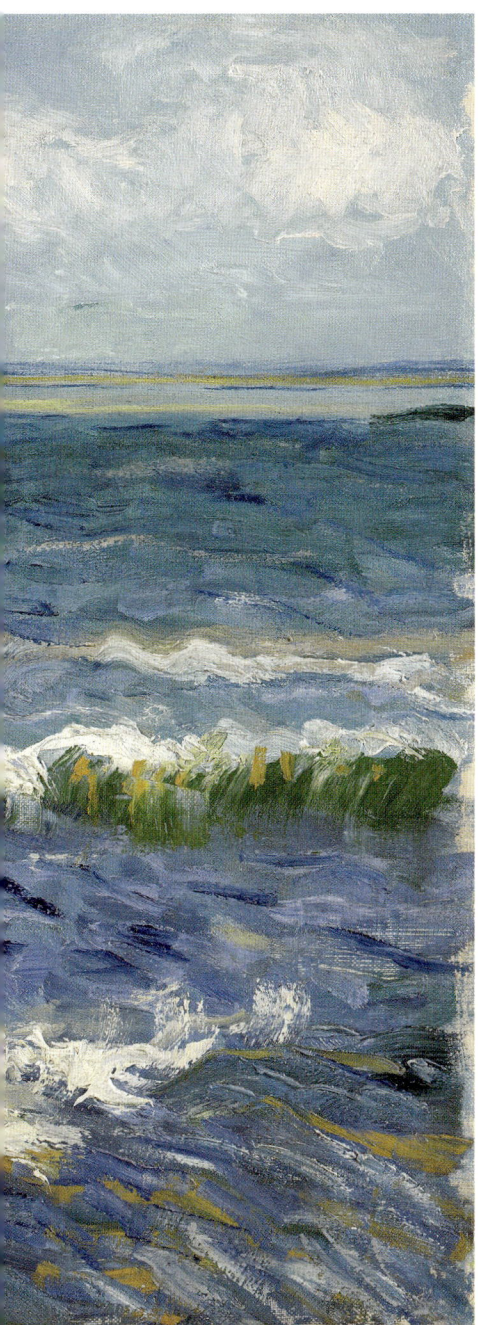

Seascape near Les Saintes-Maries-de-la-Mer, 1888

exchanged the comma- or dot-like brush strokes of the Impressionists and Pointillists with which he experimented in Paris for a new way of applying pigment with swirls and broad strokes of contrasting colours.

Meanwhile his poor health gave him no peace, he was agonised by toothache and a weak stomach, but above all he felt isolated in the new environment. Arles offered little diversion, especially from homesickness. The Provençal dialect was new to him and he frequently went for days without exchanging a word with anyone. His hope of meeting art lovers and artist colleagues in the south had not been fulfilled.

So he devoted himself completely to his work, though he did adopt a few 'cautionary rules' for his health in that he ate more regularly and drank less regularly, got an adequate amount of sleep and supplied himself with reasonable clothing. Now and again he even forced himself to take a brief pause from painting, all of this in order "to be able to persevere in the long run and work regularly". Yet he cannot have followed his rules too religiously, for he once wrote to his brother that he had survived for five days on little more than bread and coffee. Painting came first and he sometimes spent more on paints and canvas than on food. His lifestyle may not have been solely responsible for the delusions that set in in the south of France, but it was hardly beneficial given his already weak constitution.

In the Southern Atelier

In May van Gogh had already rented an atelier in a corner building on the central Place Lamartine. He envisioned that the artists' cooperative he dreamt of would live in the Yellow House and in fact he soon heard that his painter friend Paul Gauguin planned to join him. Vincent greatly admired the artist he had come to know in Paris. He immediately worked out how the atelier house, in which he was soon living as well, could be rearranged for Gauguin and himself. In a complete redecoration of his new home in Arles he furnished the nicest room as a guest room, purchasing beds, a stove, and drawing tables—not without a guilty conscience inasmuch as Theo would be paying for them as well. By September the house and atelier were ready for Gauguin's arrival. Over the summer van Gogh had produced a number of paintings with an eye towards them decorating his colleague's future room. Among them was the series featuring sunflowers, which would later become Vincent van Gogh's best-known motif.

It finally seemed that his dream of a painters' colony in Provence was coming true. In October 1888, after months of promises and cancellations, Gauguin arrived at last and their working together in the 'atelier du Midi' could begin. Van Gogh experimented with Gauguin's flat way of painting, marvelled at the other man's reliance on his imagination and tried to work more imaginatively himself. Gauguin, in turn, joined van Gogh now and again in painting outdoors. Although their association lasted only two months and the artists'

cooperative was hardly realised, this period in the two painters' work was significant. But their living together was not a success for long, they were too different and conflicts—in part fuelled by excessive alcohol consumption—became more frequent. A quarrel on December 23 escalated to the point that Gauguin stormed out of the house. Vincent suffered a psychotic attack during which he mutilated his ear. He cut off a portion of the earlobe that he then carried to a local prostitute's. After he returned to the Yellow House the postman, his friend Joseph Roulin, found him and summoned a policeman who committed him to hospital.

Gauguin telegraphed Theo telling him he needed to come, but left Provence immediately after the incident. When Theo arrived Vincent tried to reassure his brother: the attack was only something that happens to an artist who overreaches himself. He later wrote: "But to get to the brilliant yellow I managed to produce this summer it all had to be somehow driven to the extreme."

Van Gogh returned to the Yellow House in early January 1889. He still felt weak, but immediately resumed painting. He had abandoned his plans for an artists' community but hoped that painting would put him to rights. He also re-established contact with Gauguin following the drastic conclusion of their brief trial association. But after only a few weeks he found himself in the hospital again after another attack. He was released ten days later and once again returned to his atelier. But insomnia and delusions plagued him and he was haunted by fear of further episodes.

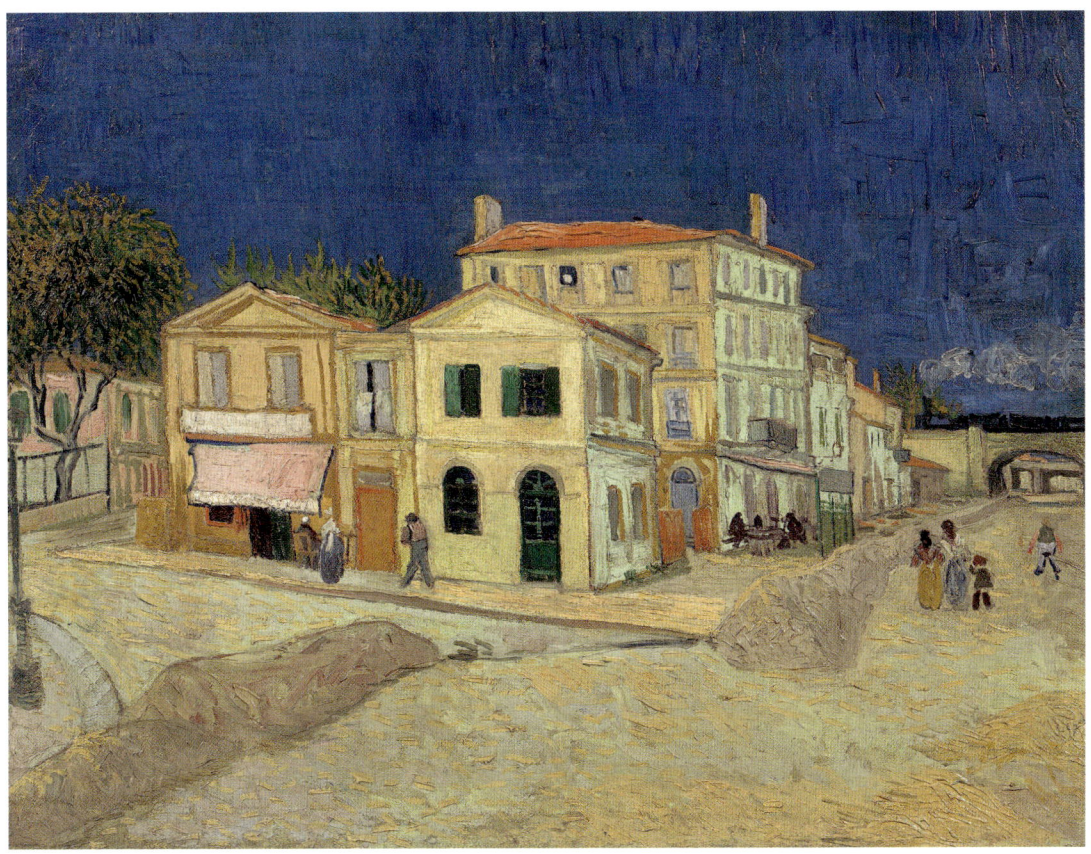

The Yellow House (The Street), 1888

Meanwhile, the artist was facing increasing hostility from the people of Arles; some of his neighbours begged the mayor to have the artist ejected from the Yellow House. Van Gogh was first detained, then spent another spell in hospital. In March his painter friend Paul Signac visited him there, which lifted his spirits. Forced to stop painting before, van Gogh even ordered new paints from his brother, planning to get back to work. Only a few weeks later he came to a decision; he would move to an asylum, where he hoped to find the peace he needed to work. He sent all his works from the Yellow House atelier to Theo in Paris. Many of them had been damaged during a spring flood, which was a severe blow, "as if not only the atelier had been destroyed, but also the studies which were meant to recall it".

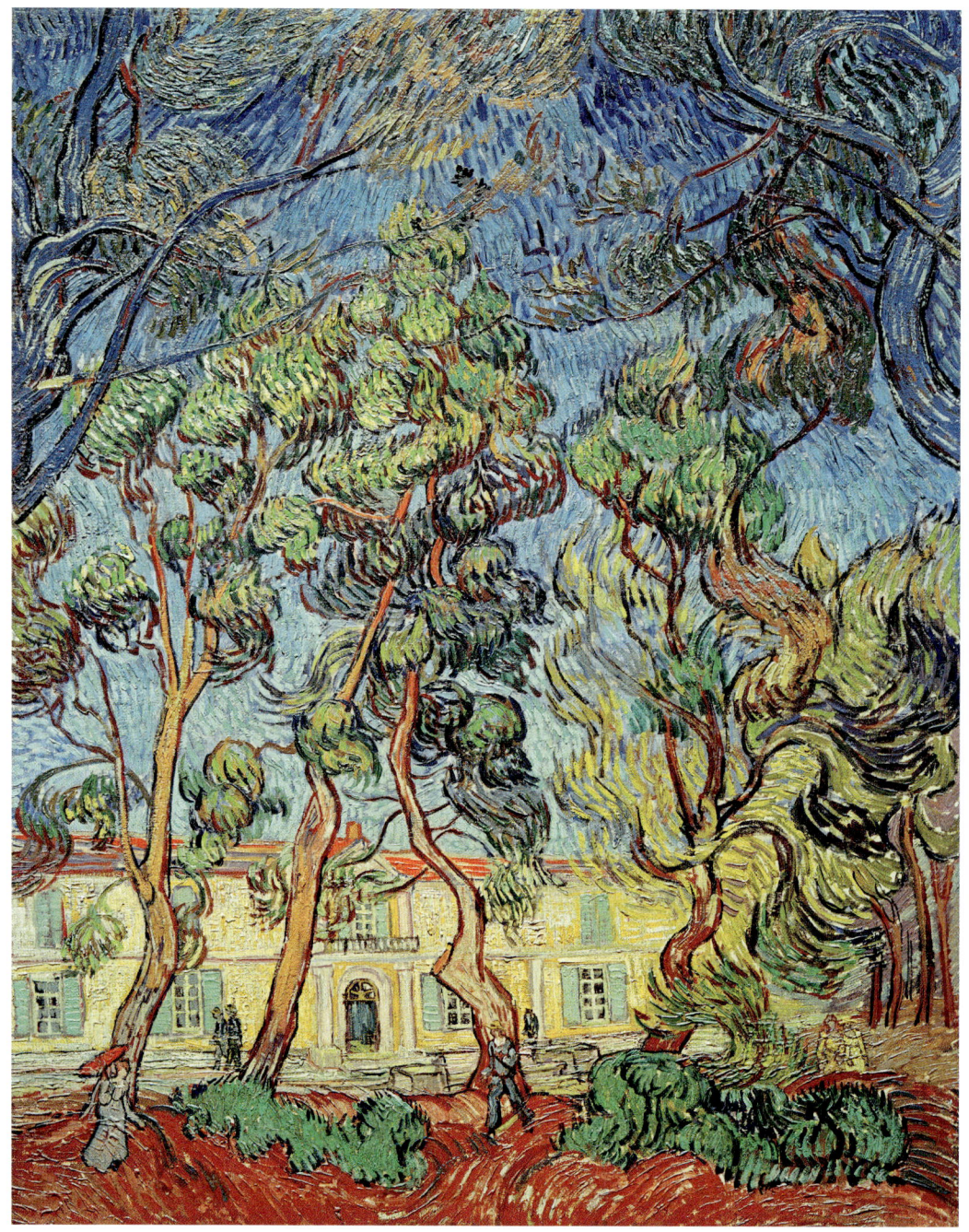

Retreat to Saint-Rémy

In May Vincent van Gogh checked himself into the Saint-Paul-de-Mausole asylum in nearby Saint-Rémy. He there suffered repeated attacks, tried to poison himself with pigments or solvents, experienced delusions, nightmares and depression. Between episodes he was still able to paint, however, even provided with a room of his own to work in, but only if watched over by a warden. In the refuge of Saint-Rémy he reworked some of his old studies and painted two large self-portraits, the entry hall and several views of the sanatorium's garden. In the summer he also worked outdoors beyond the garden area, again turning to the Provençal landscape, its fields, mountains and cypresses. In these works he introduced less glaring colours and the sharp contrasts softened. In the first months that he spent in the new environment van Gogh painted at his accustomed speed; he produced nearly 130 pictures in Saint-Rémy. Painting seemed to be promoting his recovery, which was why the renewed attacks he suffered in July struck him that much harder. His physician, Dr Peyron, suspected that he was suffering from epilepsy. A precise diagnosis is a matter of debate to this day; nothing can be determined with certainty. What is certain is that in the last two years of his life van Gogh experienced severe attacks alternating with long periods in which he was fully lucid. In the latter he painted, among other pictures, several views of the asylum's autumn garden. Vincent himself partially blamed the southern

climate for his condition and considered moving back to the north of France. But in spite of his homesickness for the north, leaving Saint-Rémy seemed too risky given his attacks. Additional episodes plagued him in the winter and for weeks at a time, unable to be outside, he had to content himself with drawing and painting after illustrations of works by other artists. As at the beginning of his artistic career, he was inspired by works of the painters Delacroix, Rembrandt and time and again Millet, whose peasant themes had inspired him early on.

Meanwhile, recognition for van Gogh's work was growing, above all in artists' circles. In the autumn of 1889 some of his pictures were included in an exhibition by the Societé des Artistes Indépendants in Paris. Theo related to his brother that he was receiving many laudatory comments and congratulations about them. In the summer the Belgian artists' group Les Vingt had already inquired whether Vincent would participate in their exhibition. Theo submitted some of his brother's paintings and Vincent's *The Red Vineyard* (page 80) was actually sold at the Brussels show. A first article about Vincent van Gogh appeared in the journal *Mercure de France* in January 1890, an enthusiastic review written by Albert Aurier. And in March of the new year he was represented in the next Paris Salon des Artistes Indépendants with ten paintings.

But his poor health gave the artist no peace, the attacks continued. Theo suggested that Vincent move back to Paris or join the artists at Pont-Aven in Brittany. In the spring, after being forced to abandon his painting for an extended period and even feeling incapable of writing letters, he finally accepted his brother's invitation to the north. In the meantime Theo had met the physician Paul Gachet, who worked in nearby Auvers, and was hoping that he could be of help to Vincent. In May 1890, after having lived in Saint-Rémy a full year, van Gogh left the asylum and visited Theo briefly in Paris. His brother had married the year before, and on 31 January Theo and his wife Johanna had become the parents of a son whom they had baptised under the names Vincent Willem. Vincent then settled in Auvers-sur-Oise. Dr Gachet received him there and the two became friends. Vincent took a room in the Auberge Ravoux and promptly accelerated his already incredible working tempo still further. Altogether he spent only nine weeks in Auvers, but in that short time painted more than seventy pictures. Most of these were landscapes, as the artist was inspired by his new surroundings. But he also painted portraits in Auvers, of Dr Gachet among others. Gachet had recommended this kind of therapy to him and van Gogh presented him with several pictures.

In July Vincent again visited his brother in Paris and then returned to Auvers. There, while out on a walk on 27 July, he shot himself in the chest with a pistol. He returned to his room, where he was found by Ravoux, the inn's proprietor. A doctor was summoned and finally Dr Gachet as well, who notified Theo. With his brother at his side Vincent died from his injury on 29 July 1890. He was buried in the cemetery at Auvers-sur-Oise. Theo van Gogh died only six months later, in January 1891 and was buried in Auvers next to his brother.

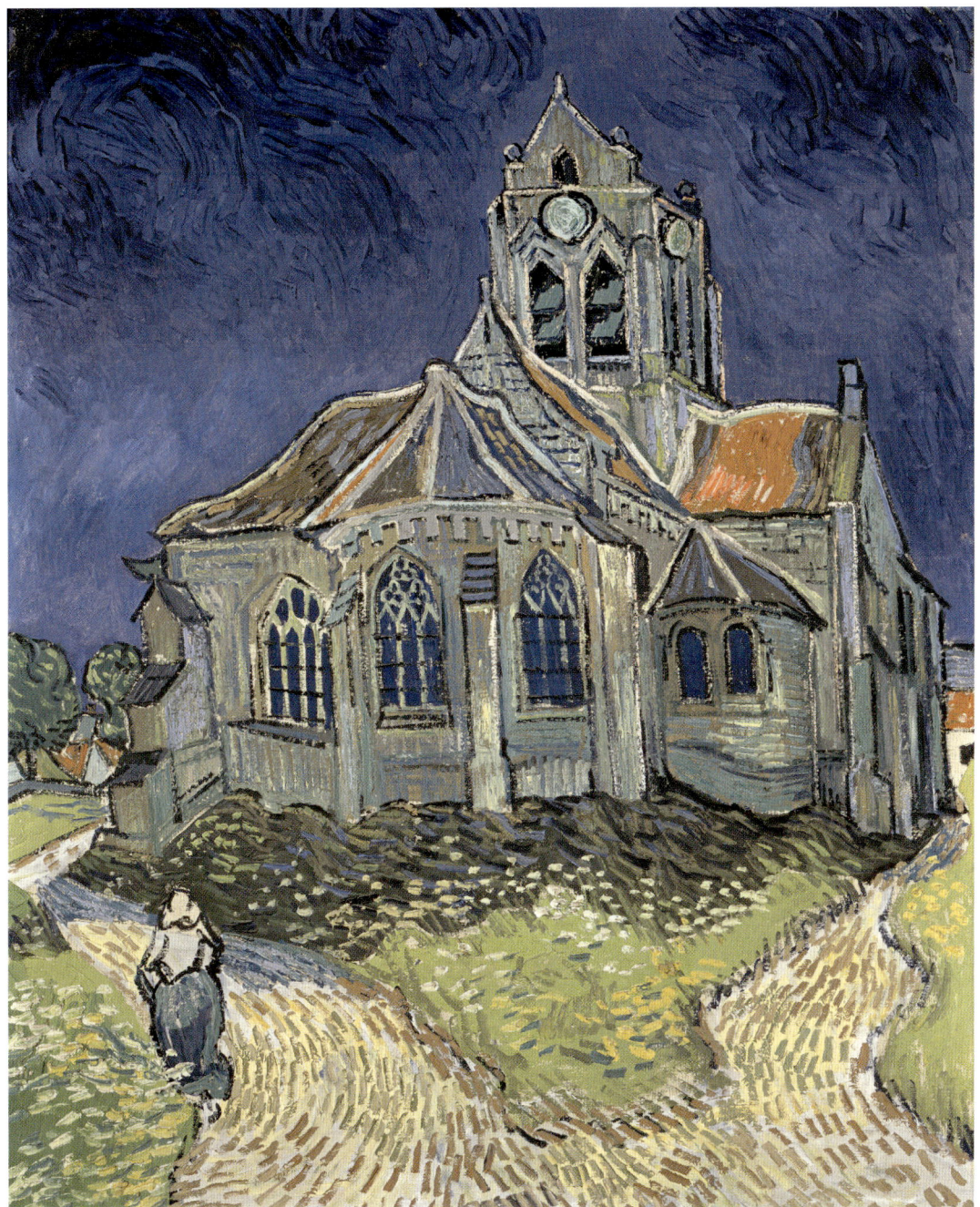

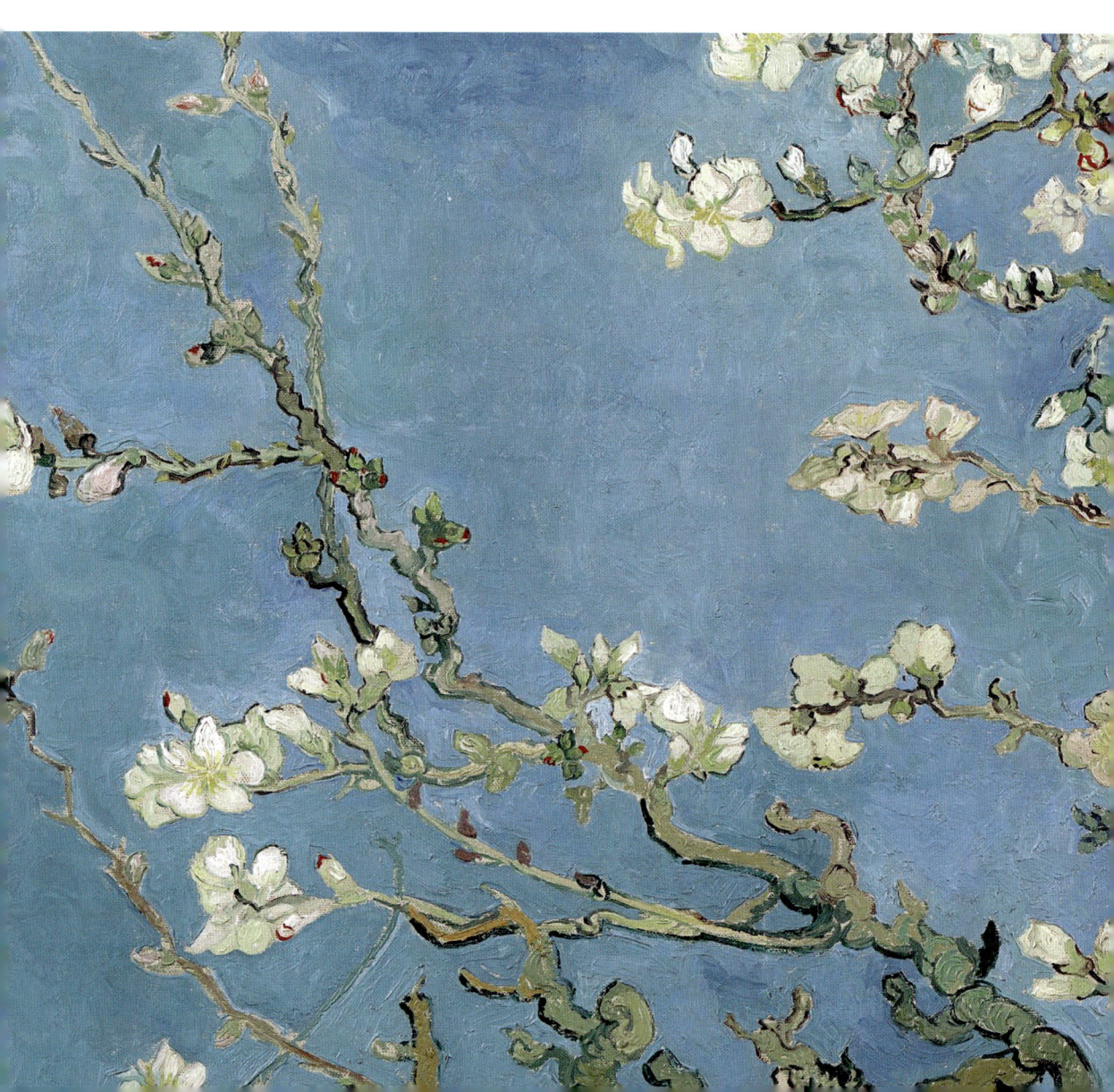

WORKS

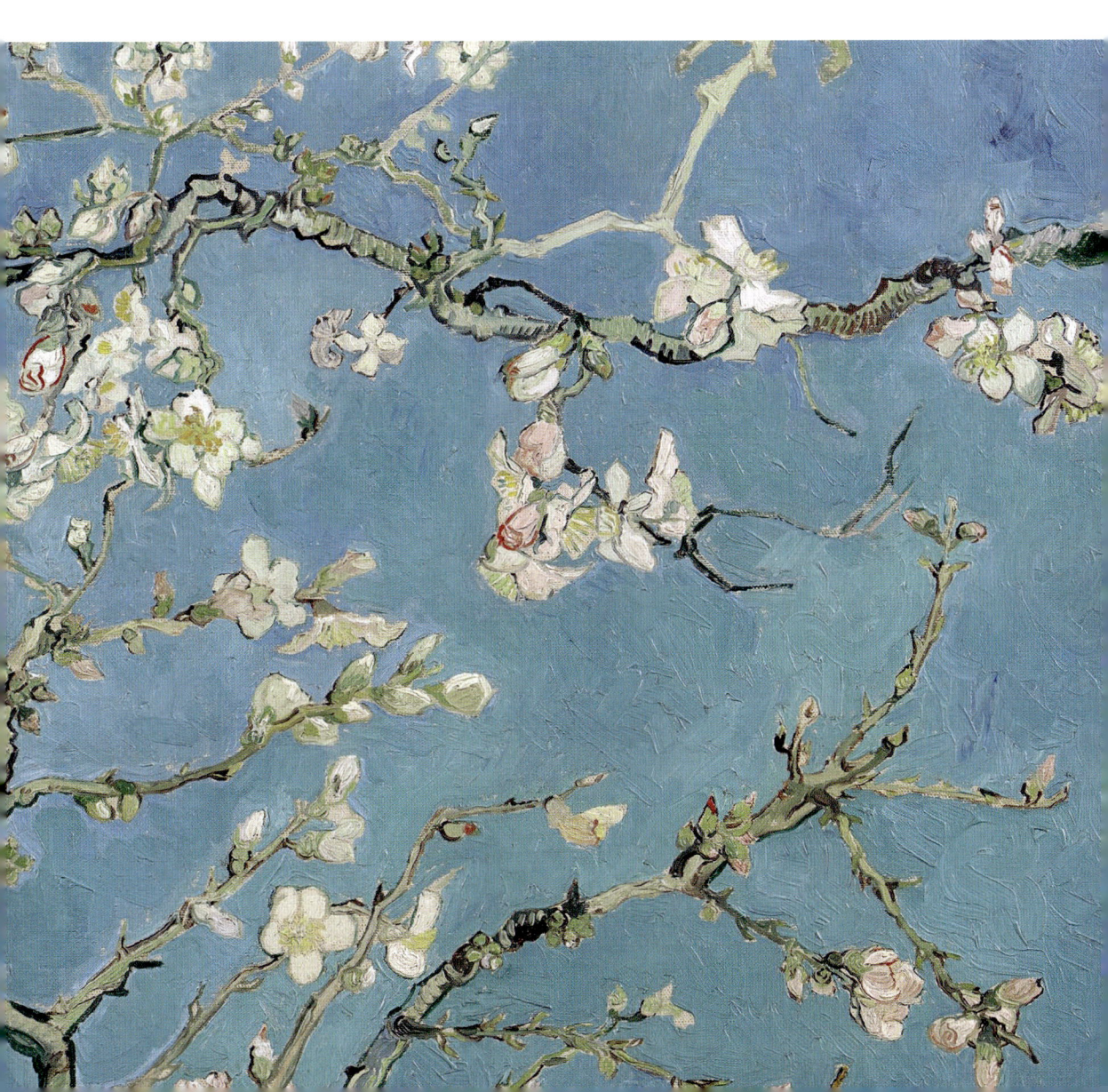

The Sower, 1881

Pencil, chalk and watercolour on paper
60.2 × 44.2 cm
Kröller-Müller Museum, Otterlo

Vincent van Gogh once wrote that drawing is "the spine of painting, the skeleton that supports all the rest". For a long time after he decided to become an artist drawing was his chief concern. He was largely self-taught, painstakingly working through his drawing textbooks page by page and returning to them time and again—he mastered the basics by himself. He studied anatomy and perspective, repeatedly copied woodcuts from his collection or sketched directly from nature. He not only drew with pencils, he also experimented with charcoal, crayons, sepia pigments and once even a bucket of water that he abruptly poured over a drawing in lithography crayon so as to then rework it in pencil. To save paper he frequently used both sides of a sheet. Even in his later years he returned frequently to drawing, at the latest whenever he had run out of paints to work with—to his great regret a common occurrence.

In the early 1880s, when he made up his mind to become an artist, the Dutchman was fully immersed in peasant life. Motifs in his often austere surroundings appealed to him. He wrote to his brother in Paris that he found everything relating to country life worth turning into pictures: "sowing grain, digging potatoes, washing turnips and all of it is picturesque, even gathering brushwood and it all has something of Montmartre about it". Van Gogh began sketching outdoors and making countless studies from which he produced finished drawings. He was often unable to find models, but in the autumn of 1881 he drew a whole series of men and women, weavers and farmers digging, sowing and ploughing. Beyond their adoption as motifs, the themes of sowing and harvesting became a constant in a metaphorical sense through his entire career. In 1882 Vincent was fully confident that "the more one sows, the more one can hope to reap".

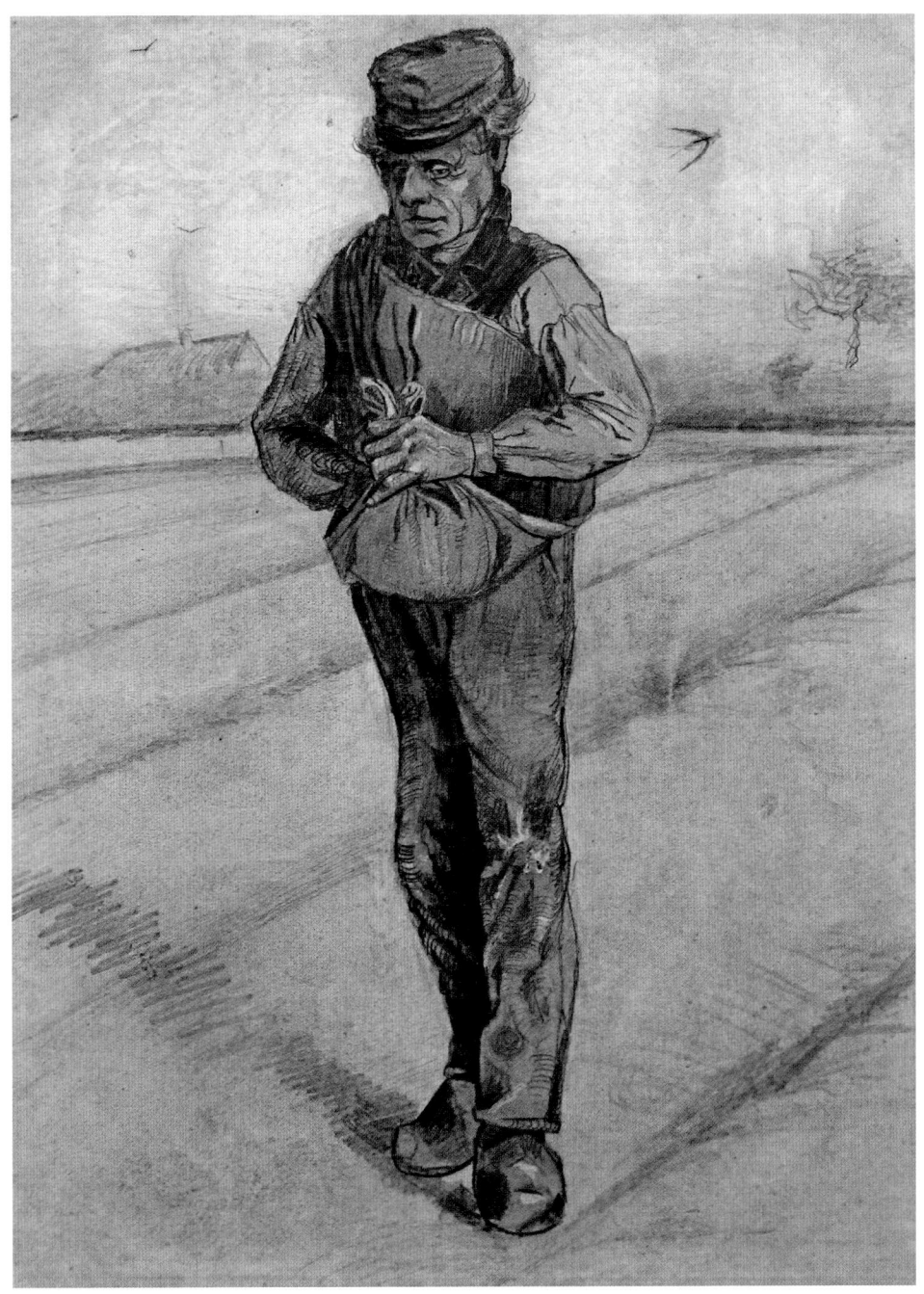

View of the Sea at Scheveningen, 1882

Oil on paper on canvas
36.4 × 51.9 cm
Van Gogh Museum, Amsterdam

For fourteen years this small view of the coast vanished from the face of the earth. It was stolen from Amsterdam's Van Gogh Museum one night but the theft was noticed only the next day and there were no traces of the culprits. With it one of van Gogh's early works was lost and one of the few that the artist had devoted to the sea in the Netherlands.

Van Gogh painted the stormy coast at Scheveningen, on the outskirts of The Hague, in August 1882. Heavy grey-blue storm clouds hang low over the breaking waves. A boat has run aground and lies in the sea. Even when painting his first pictures in oils van Gogh employed a thick application of pigment, at times not with a brush but with the paint tube itself. He painted the churning sea on the spot, for there are still grains of sand stuck in the paint. As he wrote to his brother, a second picture was so completely covered with sand that he had to scrape off the paint and start again. Working in such weather was definitely a challenge. The wind was so strong that he could hardly keep his footing. He further related that his souvenirs from Scheveningen therefore included a cold—but above all a series of drawings and this seascape, all of which were created in the open air.

After the theft it was unclear where the stolen painting might be. The museum offered a reward, but even that brought no answers. The two thieves were finally captured three years later, but they never betrayed who they had been working for. By chance, in 2016 Italian investigators discovered this picture and another one during a house search. The second van Gogh painting had also been stolen, a picture of the village church at Nuenen. Both works have now been restored to their former locations in the Van Gogh Museum.

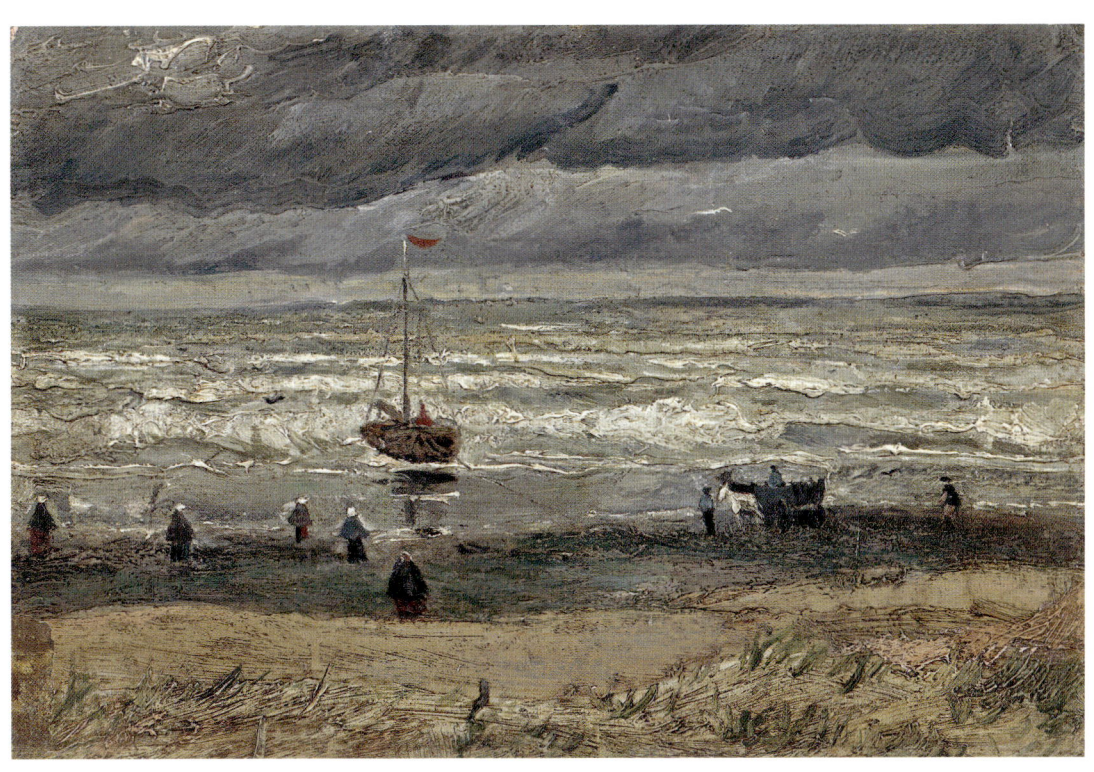

Page from a letter with a man pulling a harrow, 28 October 1883

Pencil and pen and ink on paper
20.9 × 26.7 cm
Van Gogh Museum, Amsterdam

Vincent was an enthusiastic correspondent. It is assumed that he wrote around 2,000 letters, more than 900 of which survive. Most were written to Theo van Gogh, who began to support his older brother in 1880. Theo sent him money for rent and food, paid his debts to dealers in art supplies and landlords, and dispatched canvas, paints, paper and brushes from Paris. But Theo was much more than just a financial support; for many years he was Vincent's sole confidant. And when the painter was ill, a word from Theo was twice as meaningful: ". . . for I assure you that an affectionate letter from you does me more good than my pills etc.".

Whenever Vincent was about to venture on a new painting idea he would provide Theo with an impression of it in advance, often in the form of a small sketch. Sometimes he would send his "krabbels", his 'scribbles' as Vincent himself called most of his sketches, on separate sheets but most were added between, below and beside lines of text. He sketched landscapes in his letters just as diligently as figure studies. When working with watercolours, these also found their way into his letters. But coloured drawings were the exception, he mostly drew them with a quill. This was the case in the sketch of a man pulling a harrow across a field behind him. The drawing occupies the bottom third of a sheet in a letter he sent to Theo in October 1883. He had previously reported to his brother about his progress as a figure painter and his fondness for drawing from real models.

With his letter drawings Vincent gave his brother insights into his artistic progress, whether dealing with new motifs, details of colour theory or painting techniques. He sent many of the sketches hoping to hear whether his brother considered his idea marketable. Selling his work, keeping himself above water without Theo's help, was soon Vincent's fondest wish: "I have had no 'guidance', no 'instruction' so to speak, from others, but rather taught myself and it is no wonder that my kind of execution is different when considered on a superficial level; but that is no reason why my works should remain unsaleable."

om een half jaar moedeloosheid te veroorzaken
waarna men toch eindelyk ziet dat men niet zich
had moeten laten desorienteeren –
Van twee personen ken ik den zielstryd tusschen
het ik ben schilder en ik ben geen schilder.
Van Rappard en van myzelf – een stryd soms bang
een stryd die juist is dat wat het onderscheid is tusschen
ons en zekere anderen die minder serieus het opnemen
voor ons zelf hebben wy het soms beroerd aan 't eind
eener melankolie een beetje licht een beetje vooruitgang
zekere anderen hebben minder stryd maar werken
misschien makkelyker doch het persoonlyk
karakter ontwikkelt zich ook minder. Gy zoudt ook
dien stryd hebben en ik zeg weet van uw zelf dat gy
het zwaar om door lui die zonder twyfel magty beste
intenties hebben van streek te worden gebragt –
Als iets en u zelf zegt u gy zyt geen schilder – schilder
dan juist Kerel en die dan bedaart ook maar
slechts daardoor – Wie als hy dat voelt gaat naar
vrienden en zyn nood klaagt verliest iets van
zyn mannelykheid iets van het beste wat in hem is –
uw vrienden kunnen slechts zyn degenen die
zelf daartegen vechten door eigen voorbeeld van
actie active in u opwekken –

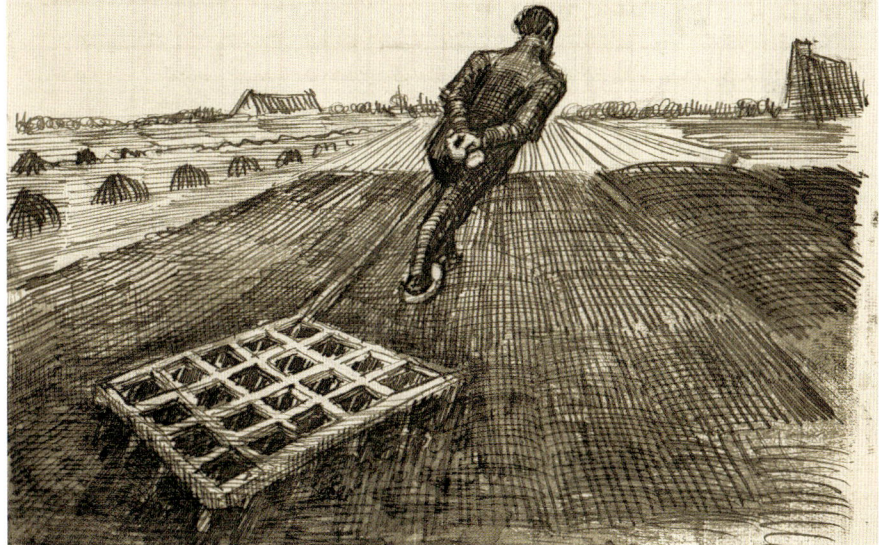

Avenue of Poplars in Autumn, 1884

Oil on canvas
99 × 65.7 cm
Van Gogh Museum, Amsterdam

Van Gogh spent the year 1884 with his parents in Nuenen, a small village near Eindhoven. He had moved back in with them at New Year's and set up an atelier in a small laundry room in their house. Vincent painted the rural life of his homeland, the village church, the weavers and farmers, the flat landscape. This road lined with poplars appealed to him and in the autumn he devoted several paintings to the motif. He frequently wrote to Theo how much he treasured this season for his painting—the leaves changing colours and falling, the fading light of days growing ever shorter.

The artist described even this large canvas as a mere study, not a finished picture— he still considered himself far from his goal. But in contrast to previous years van Gogh now at least thought of himself as a painter. Accordingly, he also wanted the arrangement he had made with Theo to be clarified. His brother had supported him even before, but in the early summer of 1884, after a few heated letters, the two were in agreement: in future Vincent would sell his works to his brother so Theo's financial support was in fact payment for pictures received. So from then on at irregular intervals smaller or larger packages and rolls with drawings and oil paintings were sent off to Paris, where Theo lived and operated an art gallery. In previous years Vincent had often complained that Theo had still not sold any of his works. Now, under the new agreement, the art dealer himself would be out of pocket if Vincent's paintings and drawings still failed to find buyers. And as Vincent openly admitted, he even counted his brother in among all the feckless art dealers who were uninterested in his works: "My spiteful outbreaks are bullets meant not for you, as you are my brother, but to the company in which you now find yourself in general."

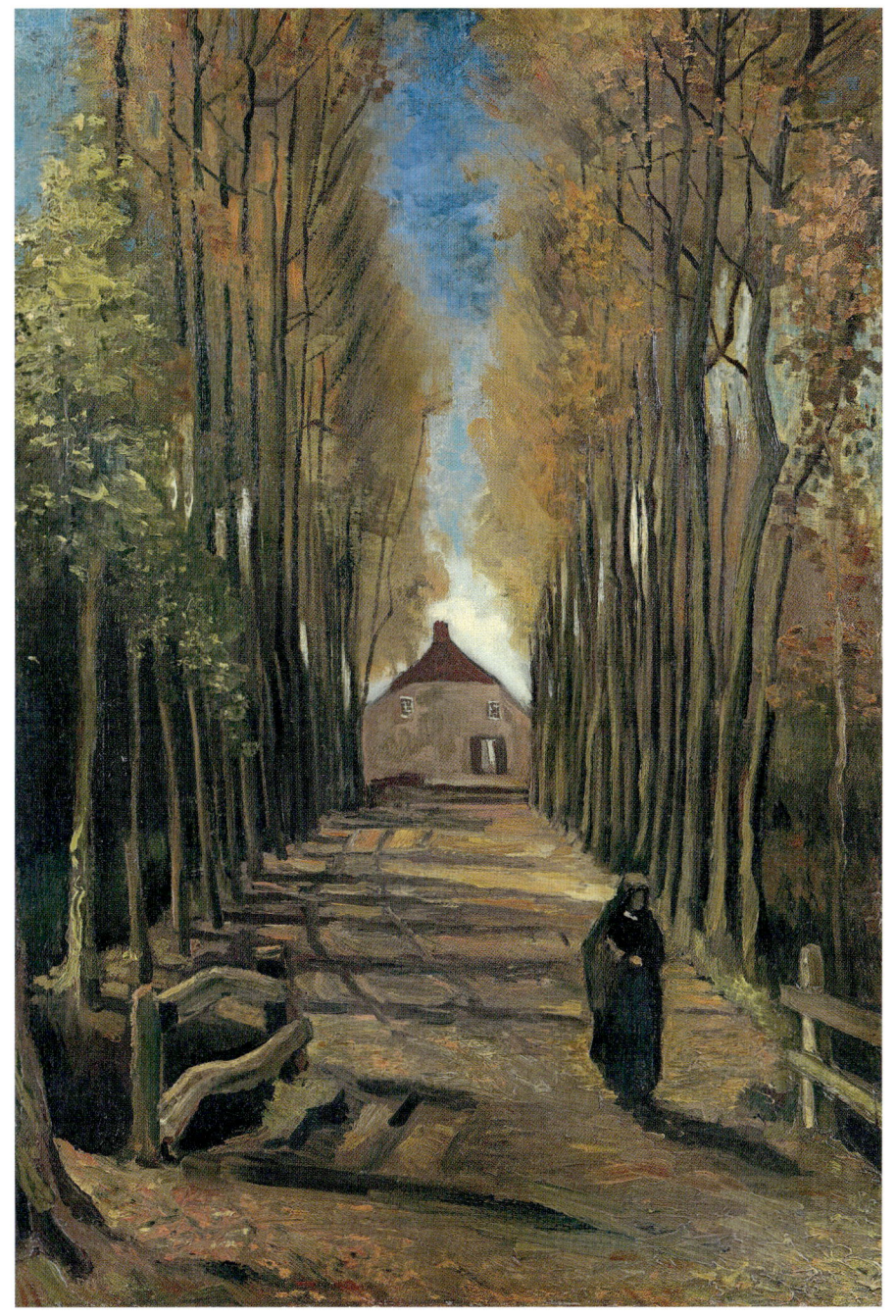

The Potato Eaters, 1885

Oil on canvas
82 × 114 cm
Van Gogh Museum, Amsterdam

In the late spring of 1885 van Gogh started to work on his first large-format oil painting. For two years he had drawn and painted the peasants in his North Brabant homeland again and again and the large work features several of them, a family gathered together for supper. The scene is dimly lit by the oil lamp hanging above the table—the only source of light in the entire picture. The play of light and shadow is one notable feature of the work, the composition with its five figures the other: with his ambitious painting van Gogh wanted to show that he was at last turning into a good figure painter.

In the preceding months he made dozens of preliminary drawings for his painting, whole series of studies not only of the figures' crude faces and knobbly hands but also of the kettle, that repeatedly changed its location as he worked out the composition, and even the placement of the potato fork. Van Gogh painted the evening scene in dark, earthy tones; he was determined to produce a realistic picture of farming people, without idealising reality. For the faces of his figures, for example, he aimed for the "colour of a really dusty potato, unpeeled of course".

Vincent was satisfied with the result but his peasant picture earned him a fair amount of criticism, above all from artist colleagues. The proportions were unconvincing, the figures too ugly, the choice of such dingy colours made it unmarketable. Theo was also not always convinced by his brother's peasant themes. Vincent stood up to him: "I've had the threads of this fabric in my hands the whole winter and sought the final pattern and if it is now a cloth with a raw and rough appearance, the threads were nonetheless selected with care and according to certain rules and it could well turn out that it is a *genuine peasant picture. I know that that's what it is*."

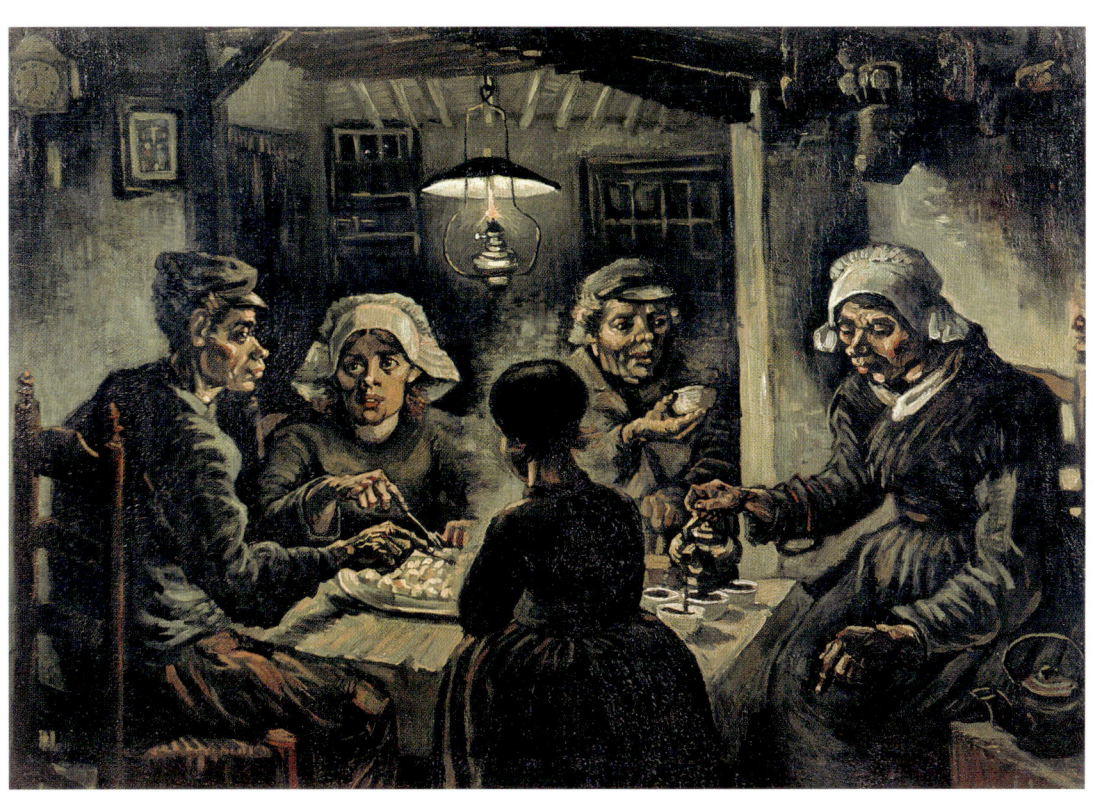

The Hill of Montmartre, 1886

Oil on canvas
38.1 × 61.1 cm
Kröller-Müller Museum, Otterlo

Van Gogh was a great champion of "much drawing and little colour", as he once put it. Yet in late 1885 he began to rework his sober, dark palette of earthy colours. The precise study of nature and reality became less important, for he now discovered something new: the power of colour. He suddenly wished to get away from the peasant painting he had pursued for so long. The "much drawing" all those years was nevertheless important, he insisted: "One begins by working one's fingers to the bone in imitation of nature and everything works the opposite way; one ends up creating something out of one's palette and nature subsequently agrees. The two contradictions go hand in hand. The drudgery, though seemingly to no avail, provides familiarity with nature, a thorough knowledge of things."

When he arrived in Paris in the spring of 1886 van Gogh began to "create out of his palette", though only hesitantly at first. He felt drawn out of doors into the neighbourhood—namely the area around the hill of Montmartre, which at that time had not yet been built up. He painted several views of the distinctly rural area that spring: it still featured windmills, fields and a few small buildings and vegetables for Paris's markets were grown in its gardens. Right around the corner from his apartment was a large stone quarry that van Gogh repeatedly pictured on canvas. In the panorama that now hangs in the Kröller-Müller Museum he was still approaching his new environment with caution in his painting; the palette, with the brownish, autumnal tones of the fields and houses, is still reminiscent of his Netherlandish paintings. But added to it are various greens and blues in the fields and sky, as well as white, with which the painter renders the low clouds on the horizon.

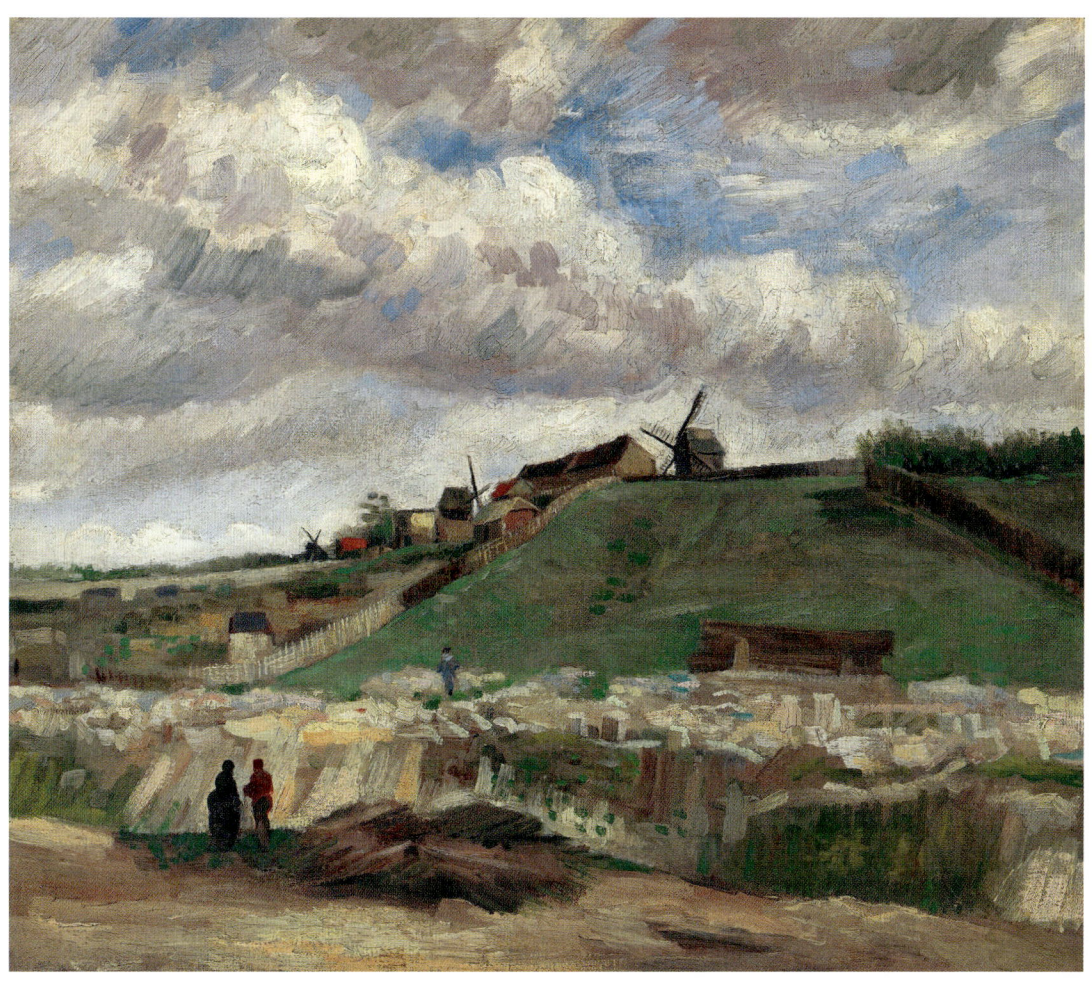

Vase with Poppies, 1886

Oil on canvas
54.6 × 45.1 cm
Wadsworth Atheneum of Art, Hartford

Within only a few weeks of his first summer in Paris van Gogh painted nearly three dozen pictures devoted exclusively to flowers. Bright red poppies and delicate blue forget-me-nots, white and pink roses, yellow chrysanthemums, blue cornflowers and dark red gladioli. Suddenly the dark colours and grey harmonies of his depictions of peasant life seem to be forgotten. In Paris he painted colour studies, as he called his pictures, and experimented with the brighter palette of the Impressionists "in order to accustom myself to colours other than grey, namely to pink, pale or bright green, bright blue, violet, yellow, orange, gorgeous red". While writing to his sister and artist colleagues about his colour experiments he painted with increasingly radiant colours, placing them together in new compositions full of contrasts. He even risked juxtapositions that further intensified his colours—blue next to orange, yellow with violet, or red and green, as here in *Vase with Poppies*. Added to this feast of colours are a whole range of other tones, varied, light, cheerful: shimmering between the green buds of the poppies is a delicate pink and on many of the wide-open blooms there is a robust orange.

The floral still lifes from the summer of 1886 represent van Gogh's breakthrough to a new way of painting. And to a new sense of himself: Vincent exhibited his studies at a few art galleries, traded works with other artists and organised shows for the "painters of the Petit Boulevard". This is what he called himself and such artist colleagues as Émile Bernard and Henri de Toulouse-Lautrec who also lived on the Boulevard de Clichy in Montmartre. In contrast to them, better-known painters exhibited at imposing addresses along the grand boulevards in the city's centre. Van Gogh showed his floral still lifes together with works of his painter friends in several exhibitions in cafés and restaurants. He ultimately hoped he would have a better chance of selling his work with the new motifs, for flower pictures were popular at the time. Many of his floral paintings also hung on the walls of their regular meeting place, the Café Le Tambourin in Montmartre: he had arranged with its owner that he would give her pictures in exchange for food and drink.

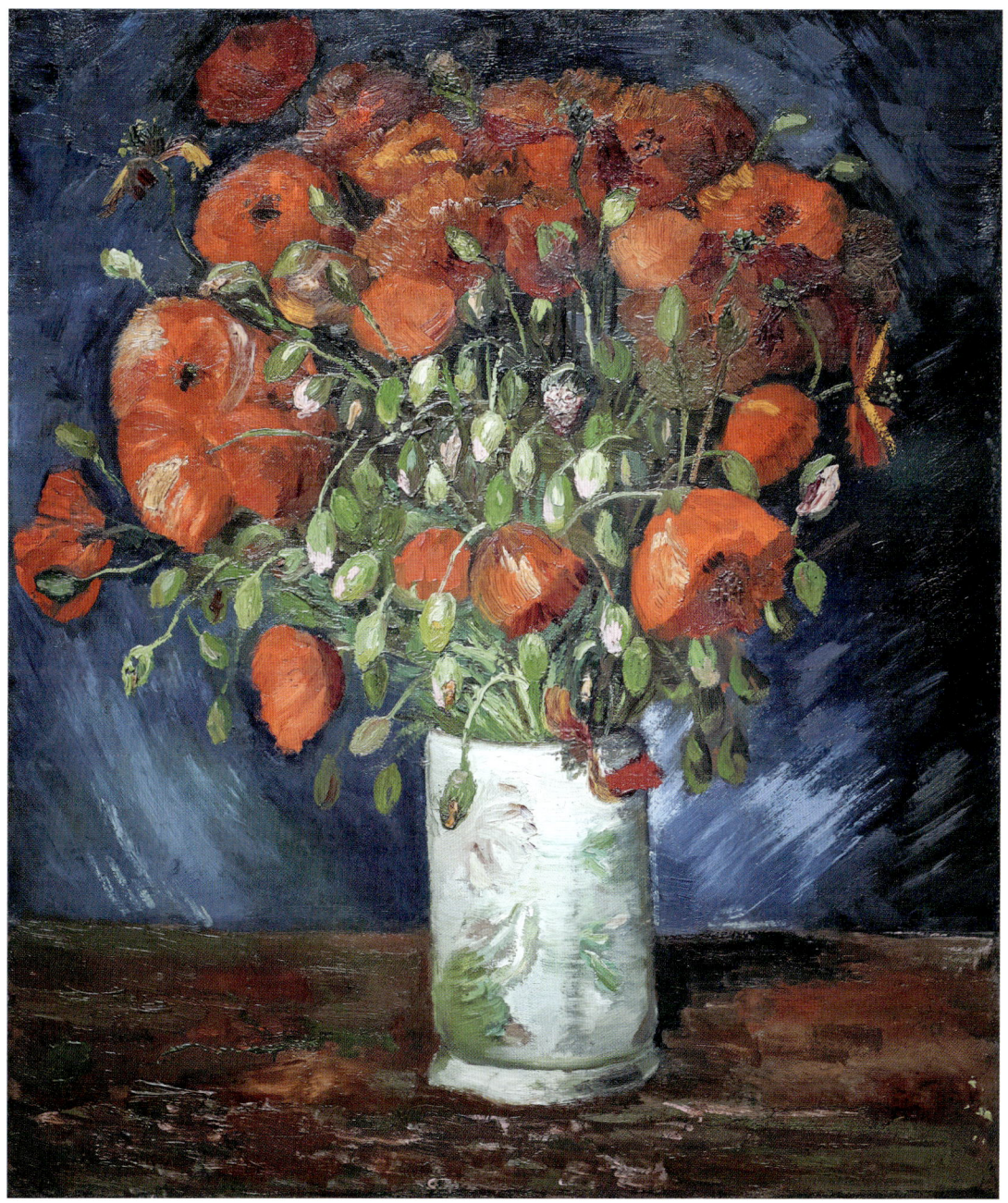

View from Theo's Apartment, 1887

Oil on canvas
45.9 × 38.1 cm
Van Gogh Museum, Amsterdam

While still in the north of Holland Vincent wrote to his brother: "Because you are in Paris, I find the idea of Paris a good one and if I were less alone that way I would also make better progress." Vincent decided to leave for Paris not only because Theo had already been living there for a long time, but also because of his need for new inspiration and the prospect of contact with other artists.

Vincent suddenly arrived in the French capital in March 1886—much to Theo's surprise. "I assume that you're not pleased about my coming to Paris immediately, otherwise you would probably have answered me." Vincent's assumption was correct. His brother was also in favour of the move, but he would have preferred to proceed less spontaneously. But that was not to be as is shown by Vincent's next 'letter', only days later, hastily written in pencil on the back of a laundry ticket, indicating that he had already arrived and requesting that Theo meet him at the Louvre.

In the next months, Vincent diligently pored over the art in Paris's museums. But the painting of his contemporaries, especially the Impressionists and Pointillists, also captivated him. Shortly after his arrival he visited the eighth and last Impressionist exhibition. Theo, after working as an art dealer in Paris for years, was now the director of a gallery in Montmartre and was fully familiar with the latest trends in art. In the summer of 1886 the two brothers moved into an apartment on the rue Lepic, very near Theo's gallery. Vincent captured the view onto the street and across the city's rooftops in a number of works. In them he experimented with the new painting techniques he was learning about. In *View from Theo's Apartment* he combines the Pointillists' dots of unmixed colour with his own freer painting style. In a letter to a female friend Theo described that view out his window: "The special thing about our apartment is that it has a wonderful view of the city through the window. In front lie the hills of Meudon, St. Cloud and so forth. Above them there is a stretch of sky almost as large as above a dune. With the different effects from variations in the sky it is a motif for I-don't-know-how-many paintings."

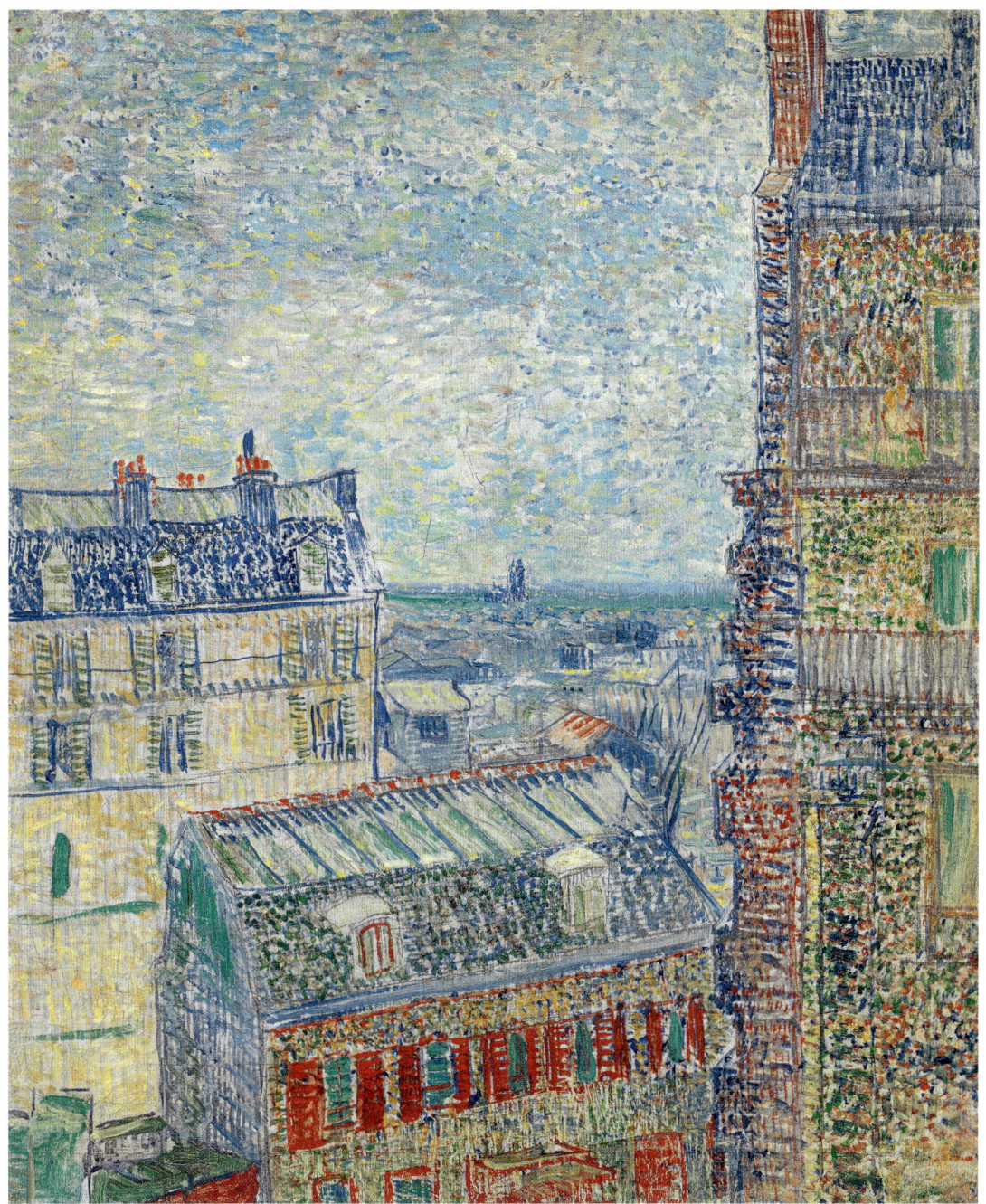

Carafe and Dish with Citrus Fruit, 1887

Oil on canvas
46.3 × 38.4 cm
Van Gogh Museum, Amsterdam

Van Gogh was now using increasingly lighter, radiant colours on his canvases. He had been in Paris for a year and become fully familiar with current trends in art at its many museums and galleries, in ateliers, at paint shops and on joint painting outings. By then he had befriended a number of artists and was exchanging works with them. Vincent was greatly inspired by the Impressionists, whose works had become well known in a whole series of exhibitions in the previous years. They frequently painted outdoors, hoping to capture the mood of a brief moment in their pictures. Since outdoor light conditions rapidly change, unlike those of an atelier, it was essential to paint swiftly. The Impressionists frequently worked with short brush strokes that remained visible after the pigment had dried. For that reason their paintings often look like sketches when viewed up close.

In Paris van Gogh experimented with the Impressionist way of painting and gradually revised his palette in favour of strong, radiant colours. Painting still lifes, whether of flowers, books, glass bottles, or fruits seemed to him an ideal way to experiment with these new painting methods and possibilities. Unlike nature and certainly models, they held still—and the light conditions remained relatively constant.

Here he tried out a new composition: the greenish tablecloth with the plate of citrus fruit lifts away from the colourful background at a diagonal. The individual brush strokes are clearly visible, though van Gogh's application of paint is so thin that in many spots the canvas shows through. In front of the colourful wallpaper stands a large glass carafe rendered with individual strokes in bottle-green, turquoise, red, white and various other tones. Showing how the wallpaper pattern is reflected in the glass was a challenge that van Gogh set himself here—and mastered. The painter signed this small still life with citrus fruit and a carafe; as always he only used his first name, to which he here added the date.

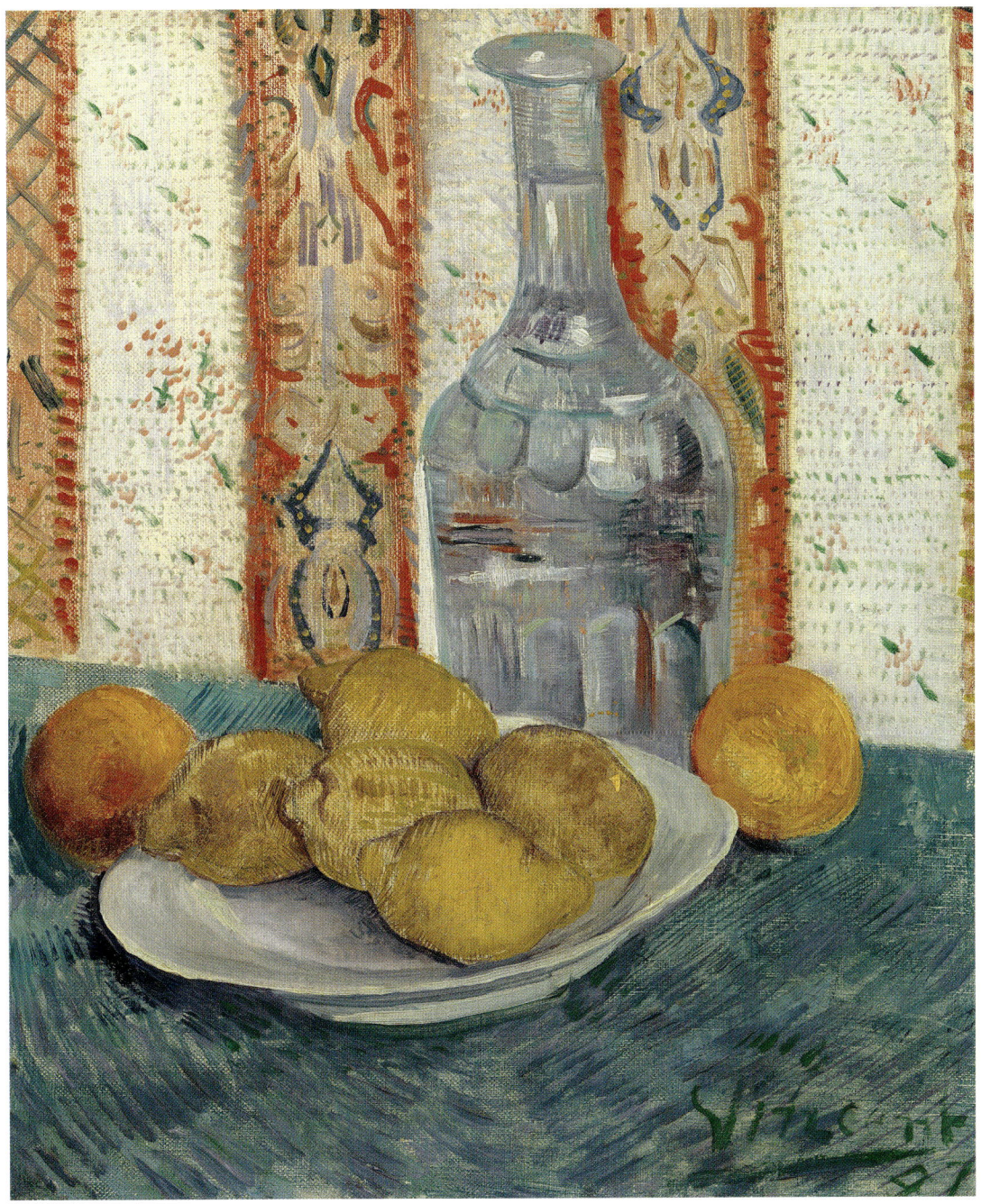

Self-Portrait, 1887

Oil on cardboard on wood
41 × 32.5 cm
The Art Institute of Chicago

During the two years that Vincent van Gogh spent in Paris he painted more than twenty self-portraits. It wasn't vanity that led him to paint himself so often but the fact that he could not afford to hire models with which to practise figure painting. Back in Antwerp he had already given up his plan to paint portraits for want of models. In Paris he resorted to his reflection in a mirror and portrayed himself. The first self-portraits were done shortly after his arrival in the spring of 1886, the last one pictures the artist standing in front of his easel with his palette in his hand. At first van Gogh remained true to the dark palette and strong shadows he had brought with him from Holland but he soon experimented with new colour values and equally new painting techniques. The small picture in Chicago dates from this time; van Gogh painted it on art cardboard rather than canvas. His manner of painting had finally taken a modern turn in the previous months. He here applies his pigments in thick dabs, a radiant green and orange, red and dark blue. The closer one looks, the clearer the many different colours become, but from a distance the individual sections appear to produce a uniform shade.

With this technique of applying pigment in small dots, or 'points', the artist Georges Seurat had made a name for himself a year before. At an Impressionist exhibition he showed his large-format painting *A Sunday Afternoon on the Island of La Grande Jatte*. Pure pigments applied close together in short strokes or simple dots were meant to blend in the eye of the beholder into an overall impression. Van Gogh, who got to know Seurat and his painter friends at their paint dealer's, tried out the Pointillist technique himself while in Paris, as in this self-portrait made up of tiny dots and strokes of colour, from which the painter's green eyes gaze out at us.

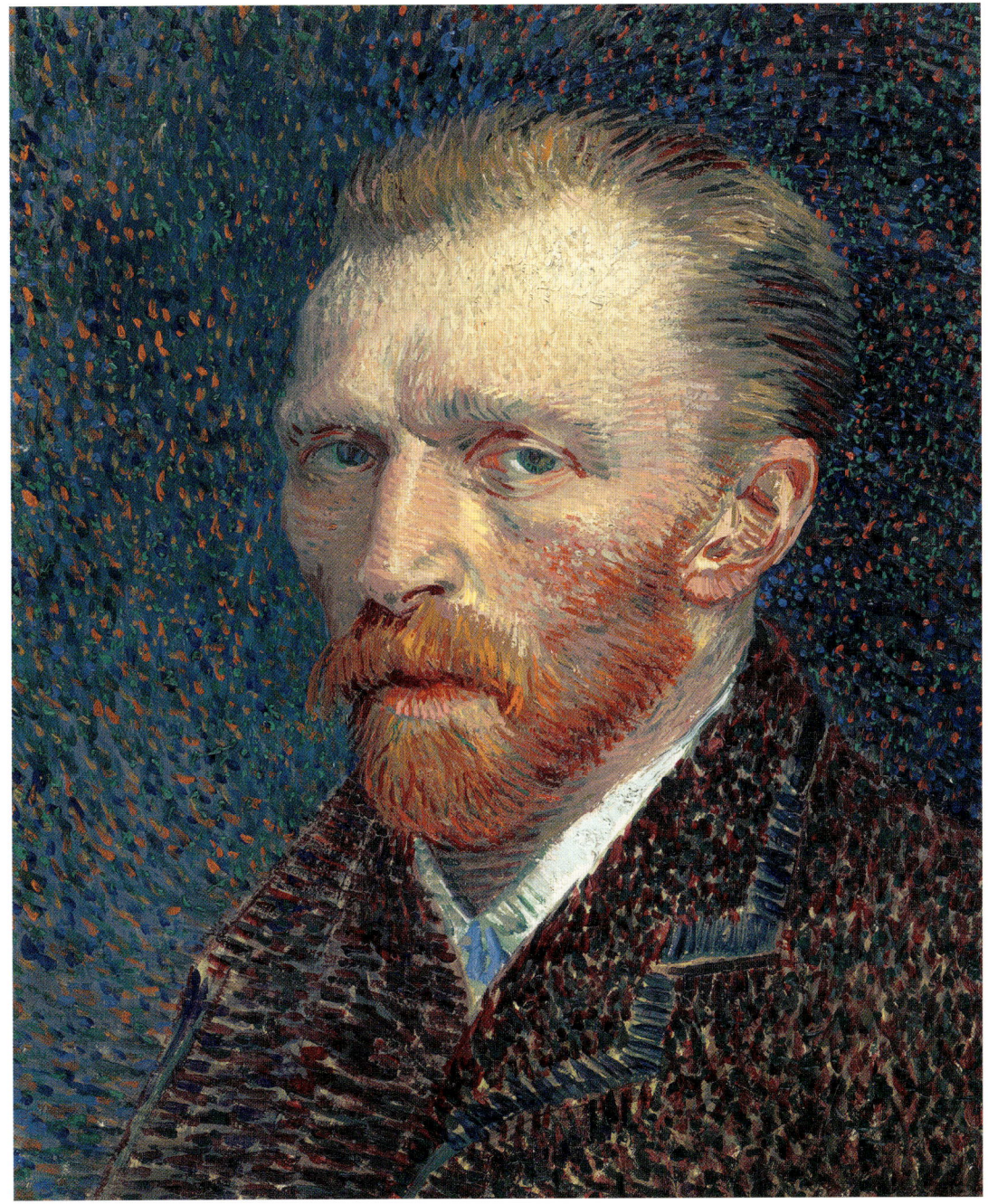

Père Tanguy, 1887/88

Oil on canvas
92 × 75 cm
Musée Rodin, Paris

In his two Paris years van Gogh painted more than 200 pictures, including this portrait of the paint dealer Père Tanguy. Julien Tanguy operated a small shop selling painting supplies in the Montmartre neighbourhood. Artists who frequented his shop prized his generous, good-hearted nature and van Gogh soon became one of them. Tanguy often accepted their paintings in exchange for pigments, brushes and canvases. His shop was a veritable meeting place for artists. Tanguy was a champion of contemporary painting, especially that of the Impressionists and Pointillists. Van Gogh was introduced to the art lover and dealer shortly after his arrival in Paris and the two became friends. At Tanguy's Vincent stocked up on the materials that he used up in great quantity in Paris and in return the paint dealer sometimes accepted his works as payment.

Van Gogh painted three portraits of Julien Tanguy and Tanguy never parted with the one shown here, which now hangs in Paris's Musée Rodin. The bearded man sits absolutely still, his large hands clasped, in front of a wall completely covered with colourful Japanese motifs. Like many of the Impressionists and Vincent himself, Tanguy was a great admirer of Japanese colour woodcuts. Works by Japanese artists, most notably Hokusai and Utamaro, began to find their way into Europe in the middle of the century—actually serving as wrapping paper for Asian wares. A craze for such art soon developed that was shared by many gallerists and collectors. Vincent was also infected with 'Japan fever' and collected a large number of the inexpensive prints. Influences from Japanese art can be seen in his own work: in Tanguy's portrait he used radiant contrasting colours in the tiny background scenes but left the picture space flat. The portrait clearly shows how greatly the artist changed his painting style during his stay in Paris.

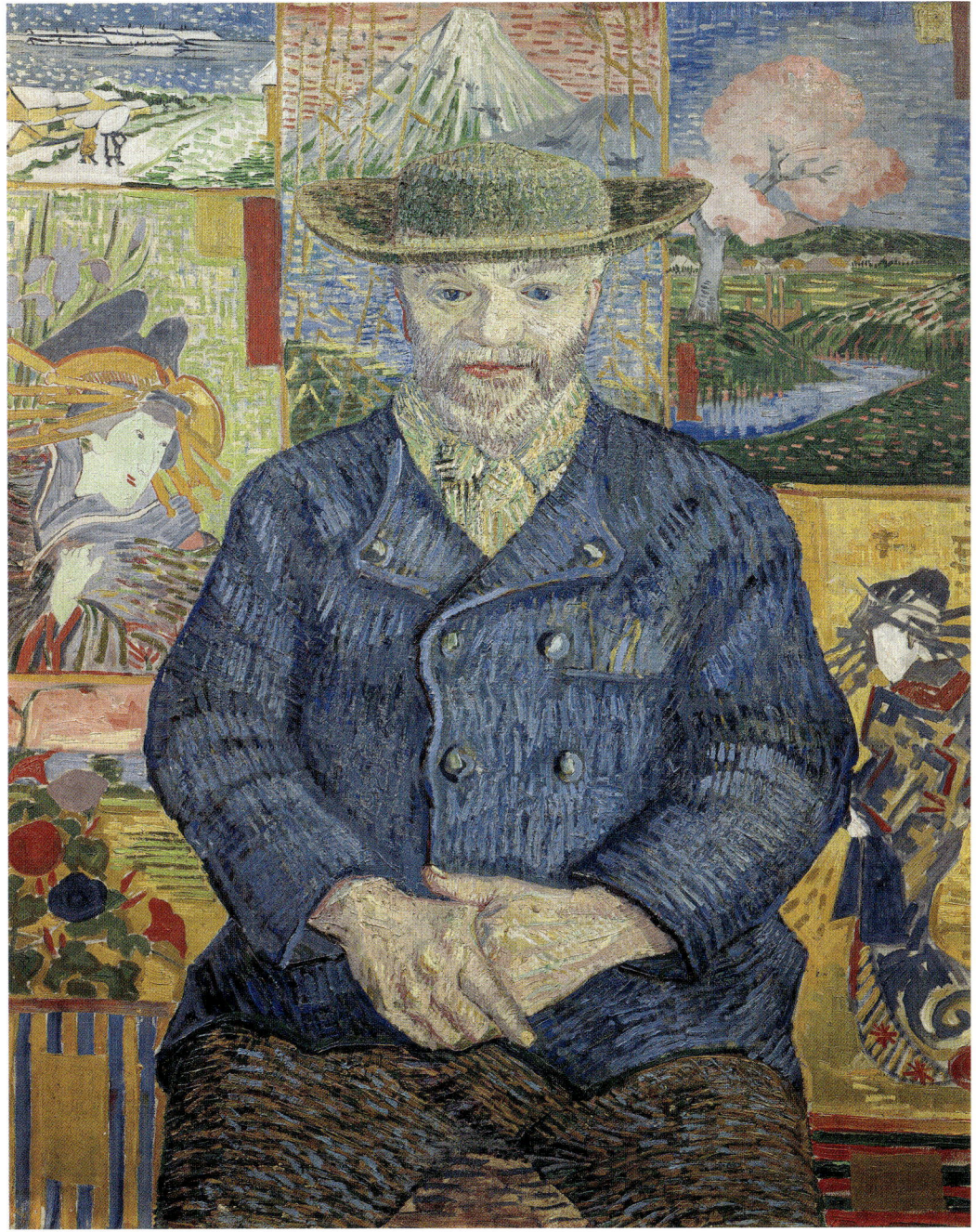

In the Café: Agostina Segatori in Le Tambourin, 1887/88

Oil on canvas
55.5 × 46.5 cm
Van Gogh Museum, Amsterdam

Agostina Segatori opened her Montmartre café on Boulevard de Clichy in March 1885. A number of artists living nearby soon became her patrons. Paul Gauguin was a regular, as were Émile Bernard and Henri de Toulouse-Lautrec. And in 1886, once van Gogh had settled in Montmartre, he likewise frequented Le Tambourin. As with most of the artists who patronised the place he would sometimes trade one of his pictures for a meal. The café walls were soon decorated with paintings, especially works by the Impressionists, who were frequent guests.

In Vincent van Gogh's portrait of the owner, painted in 1887, she is seated at one of the café tables that gave the place its name: the tabletops were actual tambourines and the waiters' trays were patterned with the same instruments. In the winter this portrait was produced Vincent and Agostina had a brief affair. He was organising an exhibition of Japanese woodcuts at Le Tambourin at the time; he not only collected the works but emulated them himself. It is possible that the painting hanging on the wall in the portrait is one of his own works based on a Japanese original. Vincent also displayed some of his floral still lifes in Segatori's café but failed to sell any. The relationship also soon ended. His brother had known about the affair first-hand, for the two men were living together. In the pre-Paris years—and afterwards—Vincent often wrote to his brother about his hapless love life. After Vincent had left the city a few months later, then in his mid-thirties, he lamented: "You see what I have found: my work; and you also see what I have not found: everything else a life should have."

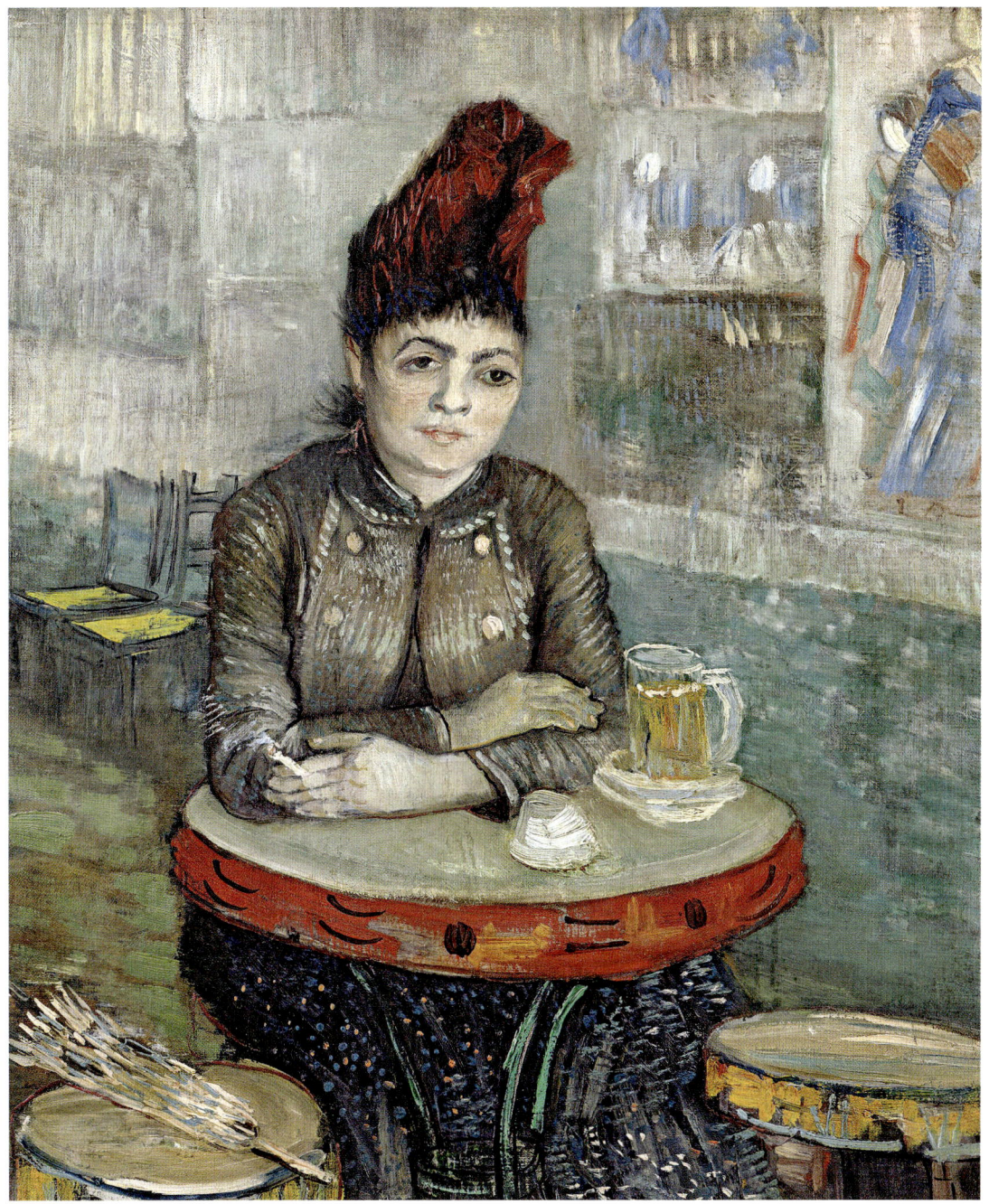

Willows at Sunset, 1888

Oil on canvas on cardboard
31.6 × 34.3 cm
Kröller-Müller Museum, Otterlo

Once he had become adept at painting van Gogh's motto was "Paint at one go, as much as possible at one go." Even in his first oil paintings he tended to apply pigment from the paint tubes themselves rather than with a brush. The resulting large paint bills were for him the eternal "downside of painting". He almost always had money worries and was in constant fear of running out of paint. After setting drawing completely aside in Paris and switching to painting in intense, radiant colours, his material requirements rocketed. He simply accepted the fact that at times their high cost left him nothing for food or clothing. In Arles, where in fifteen months he painted roughly 200 paintings, he constantly placed new orders for paint and brushes with Theo. It wasn't that Vincent was unable to stock up himself in Arles, but he begged his brother to shop at the best stores. They tended to stock better paints and they already knew him—so he could therefore hope for a decent discount on his large orders. He sent long lists to Theo from the south of France; some were not so urgent, but others included materials he needed immediately to be able to keep working. At the top of the lists for Theo during his first months in Arles stood chrome yellow and Veronese green.

At times Vincent felt guilty ordering such large quantities of paint and canvas from his brother: should he perhaps switch to drawing, which cost less? But in studies like this one he continued to familiarise himself with his new surroundings: the spring weather he met with in Arles in March 1888 called for bright yellows, warm oranges and shades of blue and red. In long powerful brush strokes a yellow sun fans across the Provençal sky.

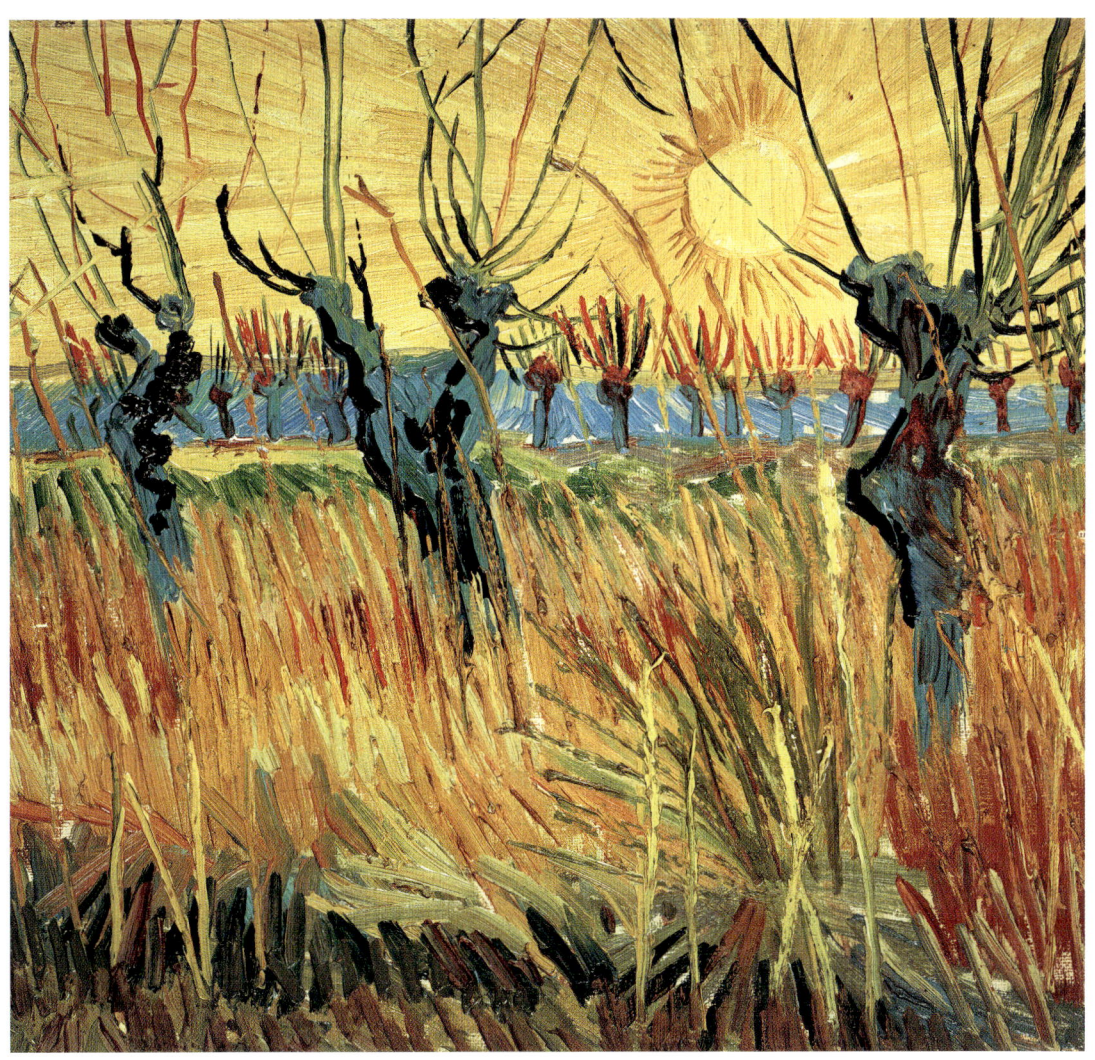

The Drawbridge, 1888

Oil on canvas
49.5 × 64 cm
Wallraf-Richartz-Museum & Fondation Corboud, Cologne

In the spring of 1888 van Gogh devoted much of his attention to the wooden drawbridge at Arles. He captured it in drawings and in several oil paintings, trying out different points of view. The motif may have reminded him of the canals and drawbridges of his North Brabant homeland. In any case, he excitedly wrote about his *Drawbridge* to his friend Émile Bernard and of course to Theo: it was the first 'picture' he had painted in his new home—as opposed to studies, his designation for most of his works.

The canvas in Cologne's Wallraf-Richartz-Museum shows the bridge from the right bank of the canal. A woman in dark clothing and carrying a parasol is passing between the wooden arches. On the left bank stand two tall cypresses, and a horse-drawn carriage has just crossed the bridge. Van Gogh painted the picture on site but carefully planned it in advance. Art conservators have discovered a first pencil drawing beneath the oil pigments as well as a detailed drawing in dark brown ink. Vincent also told his brother in detail about a wooden frame he had built that helped him capture the motif on canvas. He had drawn a pencil grid matching the one in the frame onto the canvas, then placed the frame on a wooden post in front of the motif. He could then construct his picture with the content of the individual squares. With the frame, he had already assured Theo in 1882, "one has a view of the beach or of a field or meadow *as though through a window*. The verticals and horizontals of the frame, also the diagonals and their intersection—or even a division into squares—provide fixed points with the help of which one can make a more precise drawing and locate the main lines and proportions. At least if one has a feeling for perspective. . . . Without it the frame is no use and looking through it makes one lightheaded".

The Drawbridge has been at home in Cologne for a long time; the museum's director at the time purchased the painting in 1911. Today his decision seems perfectly reasonable—what museum wouldn't like to have a van Gogh in its collection? But at the time he met with opposition from Cologne's public; many people criticised the purchase, opinions about the artist and the work differed widely. Although increasing numbers of collectors in Paris, Amsterdam and Berlin were buying his works and seeing him as a precursor of Modernism, van Gogh was still hardly represented in German museums at that time.

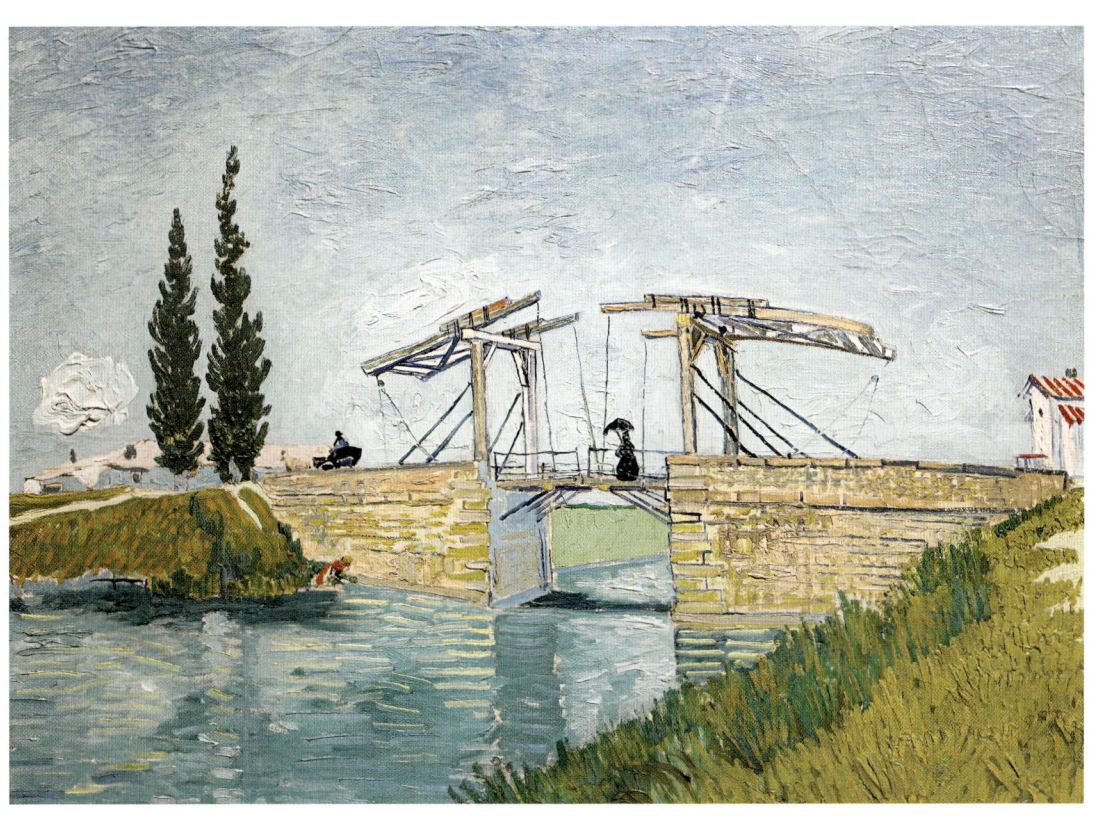

La Crau Seen from Montmajour, 1888

Pencil, reed pen and ink on paper
49 × 61 cm
Van Gogh Museum, Amsterdam

Especially in his first months in Arles, van Gogh repeatedly turned to drawing along with his painting. After a few months in Provence he wrote that he was giving "his pen free rein" and was very pleased with the results. Many of his drawings are preliminary studies for paintings, others were made because he wanted to save on materials. Occasionally he was also forced to draw because the wind made painting outdoors impossible—it didn't bother him so much when drawing. Even so, he noted that working conditions could be better: ". . . it isn't everybody who would have the patience to let himself be eaten by mosquitoes and to constantly battle against the detestable mistral". When the wind was raging in July van Gogh moved for several days in a row onto the nearby Crau Plain, which extends from Arles to the Mediterranean. He noted that its broad expanse, partially cultivated by farmers, reminded him of Holland.

In only a few days he produced five masterly large-format drawings there, among them the present view captured from a hill. He drew with a pen he had cut himself from the reeds. It produced bold, not always uniform strokes of ink that lend a painterly feel to the drawing. With horizontal and diagonal roads and boundary lines van Gogh divides the broad plain at the foot of the hill into smaller parcels. Between them in the distance one can see two farmers, on the horizon a few houses. Everything in this drawing, from the clumps of grass to the bales of hay and the trees, is made up of the small dabs of ink van Gogh placed on the paper with his pen. They are long or short, curved or straight, dot-like or stroke-like. Here again it was surely the clear lines of Japanese colour woodcuts that inspired him take on new challenges as a draughtsman.

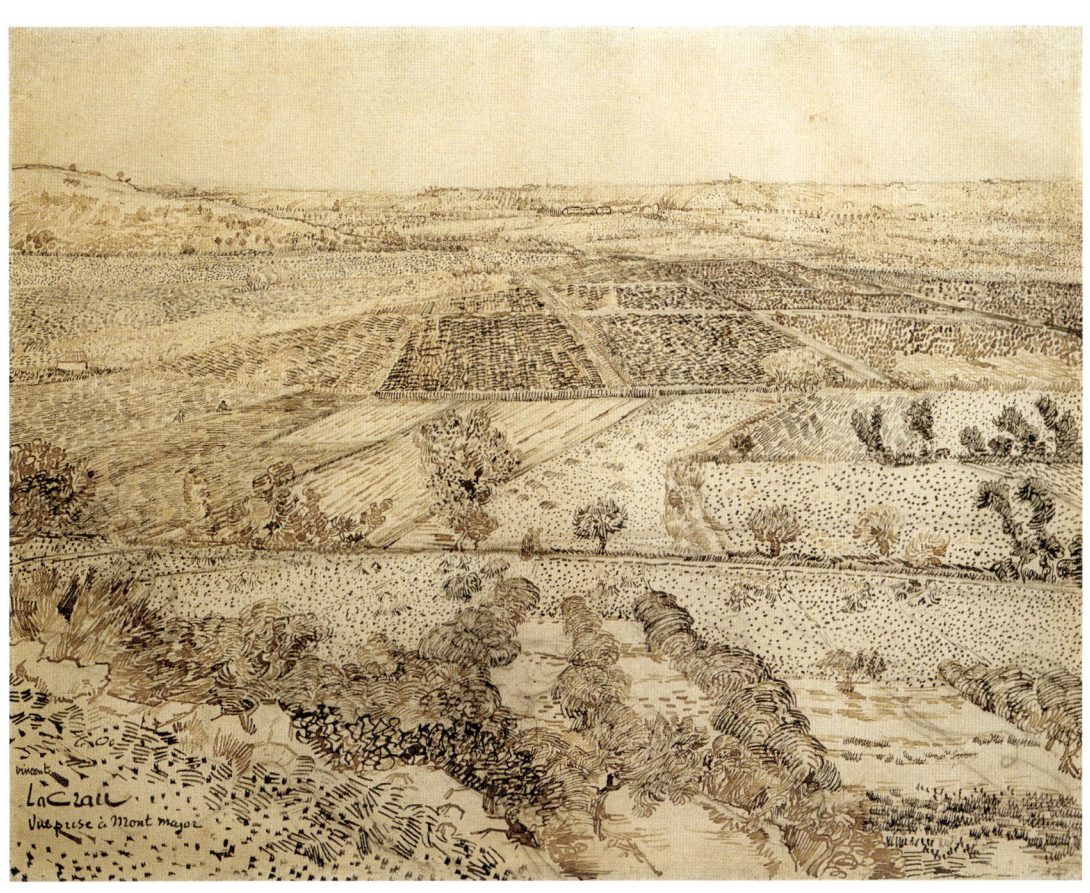

La Mousmé, 1888

Oil on canvas
73.3 × 60.3 cm
National Gallery of Art, Washington

Paris was in the midst of a 'Japan fever' when van Gogh lived there in the mid-1880s. Art and crafts from Japan fetched high prices and specialist galleries further fanned the craze. Vincent collected Japanese woodcuts himself and many of his works were inspired by them. He often bought whole stacks of them and could hardly tear himself away from the shops where they were sold. He also sampled Japanese literature, part of the widespread fascination with Japanese culture. In 1888 Pierre Loti's *Madame Chrysanthème*, a novel about a Frenchman's affair with a young Japanese woman, was all the rage. One of the book's female characters, a pretty young Japanese woman, was named Mousmé. And it was she who was the inspiration behind this portrait. But van Gogh's Mousmé, he assured his brother from Arles, was a young Provençal woman.

Van Gogh posed his young model in a chair with a curved back. She turns her face toward the viewer, her dark hair is parted in the middle and tied with a red ribbon at the back. Her face, with its dark eyes, rounded nose and slightly open mouth, is delicately modelled. In her left hand she is holding a sprig of oleander with light pink blossoms and green leaves. Here it is her brightly patterned clothing that reflects van Gogh's fondness for strong colours: the bodice of the high-necked dress features stripes of brick-red and a deep blue, with a row of round gold buttons. A white fabric projects from the neck and cuffs. The full skirt is a dark blue dotted with orange spots. The painter wrote to his brother that he had worked on this portrait for a full week: ". . . I couldn't do anything else, especially since I wasn't feeling too well. Maddening— for if I had been well I could have also painted landscapes at the same time, but in order to do a good job with my Mousmé, I had to give it my full attention."

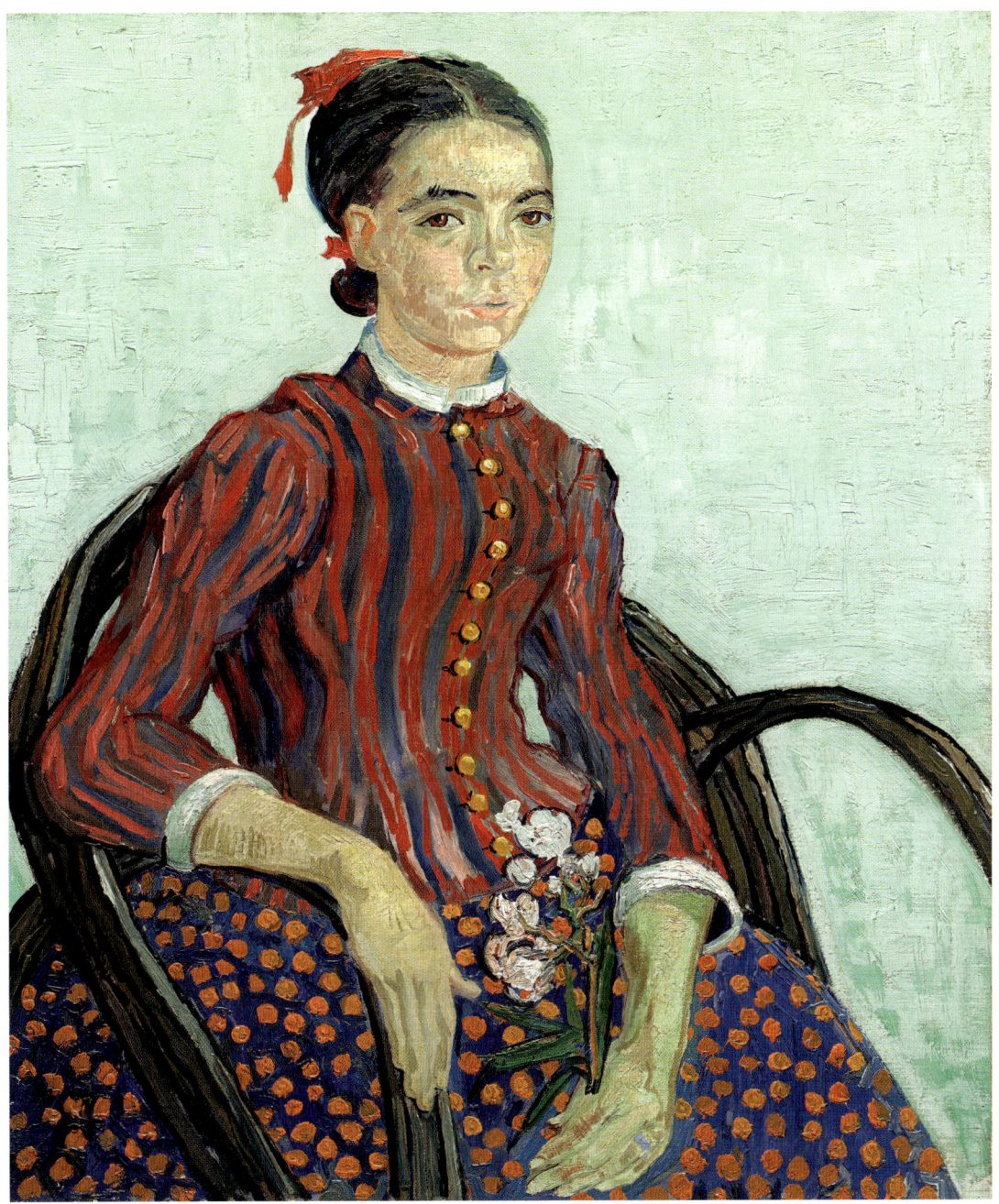

Flowering Garden, 1888

Oil on canvas
92 × 73 cm
Private collection

In Arles van Gogh followed the rhythm of nature in his paintings, producing whole series of pictures of whatever was in bloom. During the summer he was drawn to this garden in full splendour. The large canvas appears to consist solely of colours in bright tones applied in dots and short brush strokes which are placed close together. He promptly told his brother about this new motif he had painted twice, once in a tall and once in a horizontal format. In his letter, written while completely dazed by the heat of a high summer day, he included a small sketch. It reproduces the tall-format picture, with the various colours listed beside it: from the greenish blue of the sky to the black of the cypresses to the pink blossoms of the bay tree. He divides the meadow of flowers, which extends across the entire picture space, into horizontal bands: it blooms in lemon-yellow and violet, orange, red, blue and chartreuse—all colours he noted next to the sketch.

At first van Gogh's fascination with colour was purely theoretical. For months he and Theo discussed how colours work and are perceived, filling pages with their thoughts. They were not alone; in the nineteenth century any number of scientists concentrated on vision and recent findings in optics and meanwhile chemists were analysing colours, their composition and their effects. As a result, contemporary painters, most notably the Impressionists, were concerning themselves with how the human eye perceives colour. The scientific findings would play an important role when painting in the outdoors in nature and for the capturing light and colour. Another subject was widely discussed: can colours influence, even intensify each other? It soon became apparent that using colours from opposite sides of the colour wheel produced the strongest contrasts, namely red and green, blue and orange, yellow and violet. When juxtaposed, they set each other off effectively. In his pictures from Arles van Gogh enthusiastically employed such glaring contrasts.

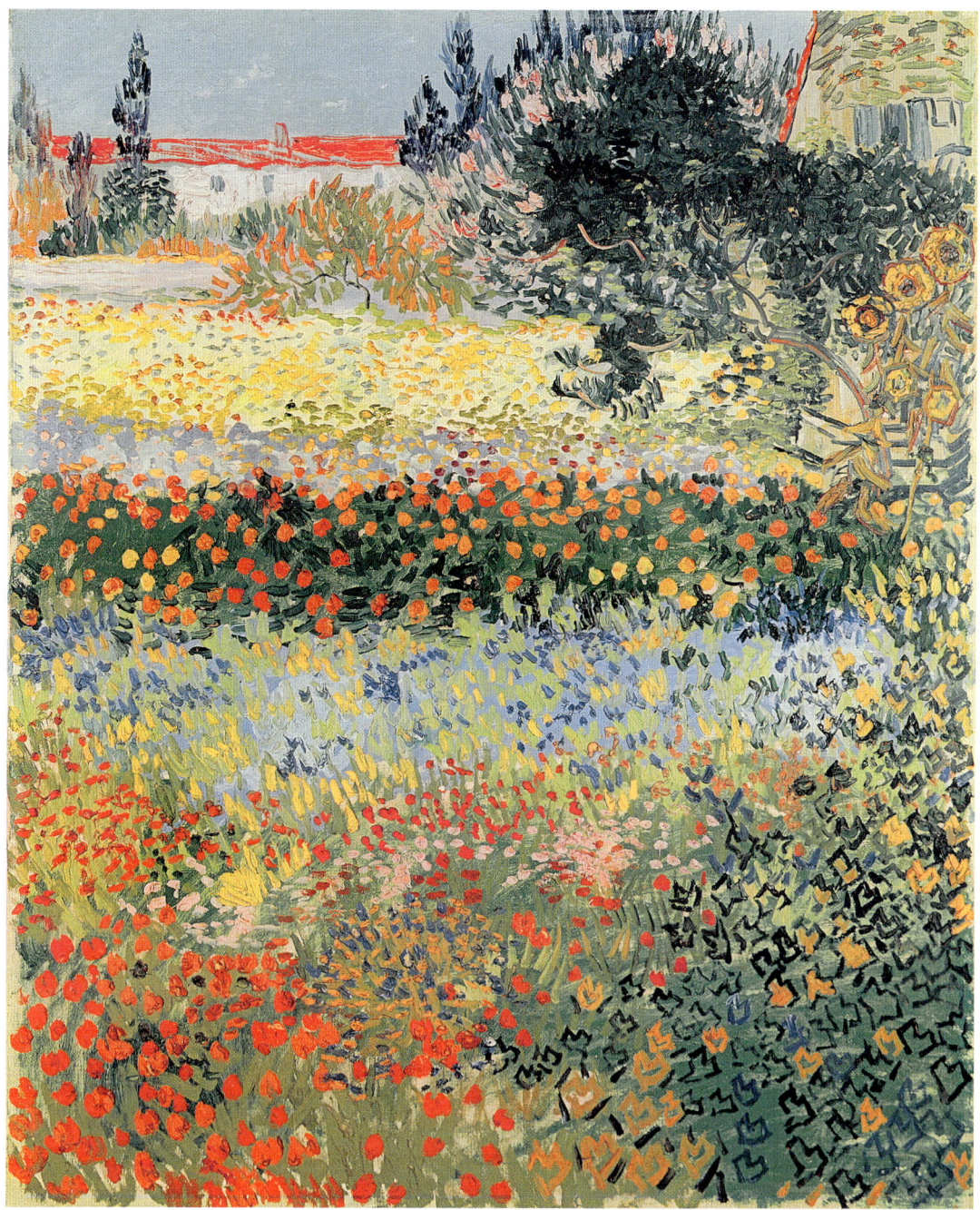

Sunflowers, 1888

Oil on canvas
92 × 73 cm
Neue Pinakothek, Munich

Vincent van Gogh's *Sunflowers* have joined the ranks of the world's most expensive paintings. A later picture from this series marked the onset of a major boom on the art market. At an auction in the late 1980s it fetched the record price of 24.75 million British pounds. The version in Munich's Neue Pinakothek was painted a few months before that one, in August 1888.

When van Gogh painted this exuberant bouquet he was dreaming about founding an artists' colony. Painter friends would work with him in Provence, in his "southern atelier". Paul Gauguin even promised to join him in Arles. Vincent greatly admired the painter, as did Theo, whose gallery represented him. Once Vincent heard from Paris that Gauguin liked his sunflower pictures he got to work furnishing the atelier house in which Gauguin would live and work with him. Large flower pictures, a full dozen of them, soon adorned the Yellow House as part of the complete redecoration. To his painter friend Émile Bernard he happily wrote: "I'm thinking of decorating my atelier with a half-dozen pictures of sunflowers—a wall decor in which unmixed and muted chrome yellows would glow against different backgrounds, blue from the palest Veronese green to royal blue, framed in narrow strips painted red-orange. An effect like Gothic church windows."

In the Munich painting the large sunflowers glow against a turquoise background that contrasts with the yellow, orange and brown tones of the flowers, vase and table. Van Gogh keeps the depiction flat so that the focus is on the colour effect. Some of the flowers are in full bloom, others wilting and dropping their petals. Van Gogh captures their different textures; long brush strokes follow the direction of the yellow petals and the green leaves and stems, while the faded blooms are composed of thick dabs and dots of pigment.

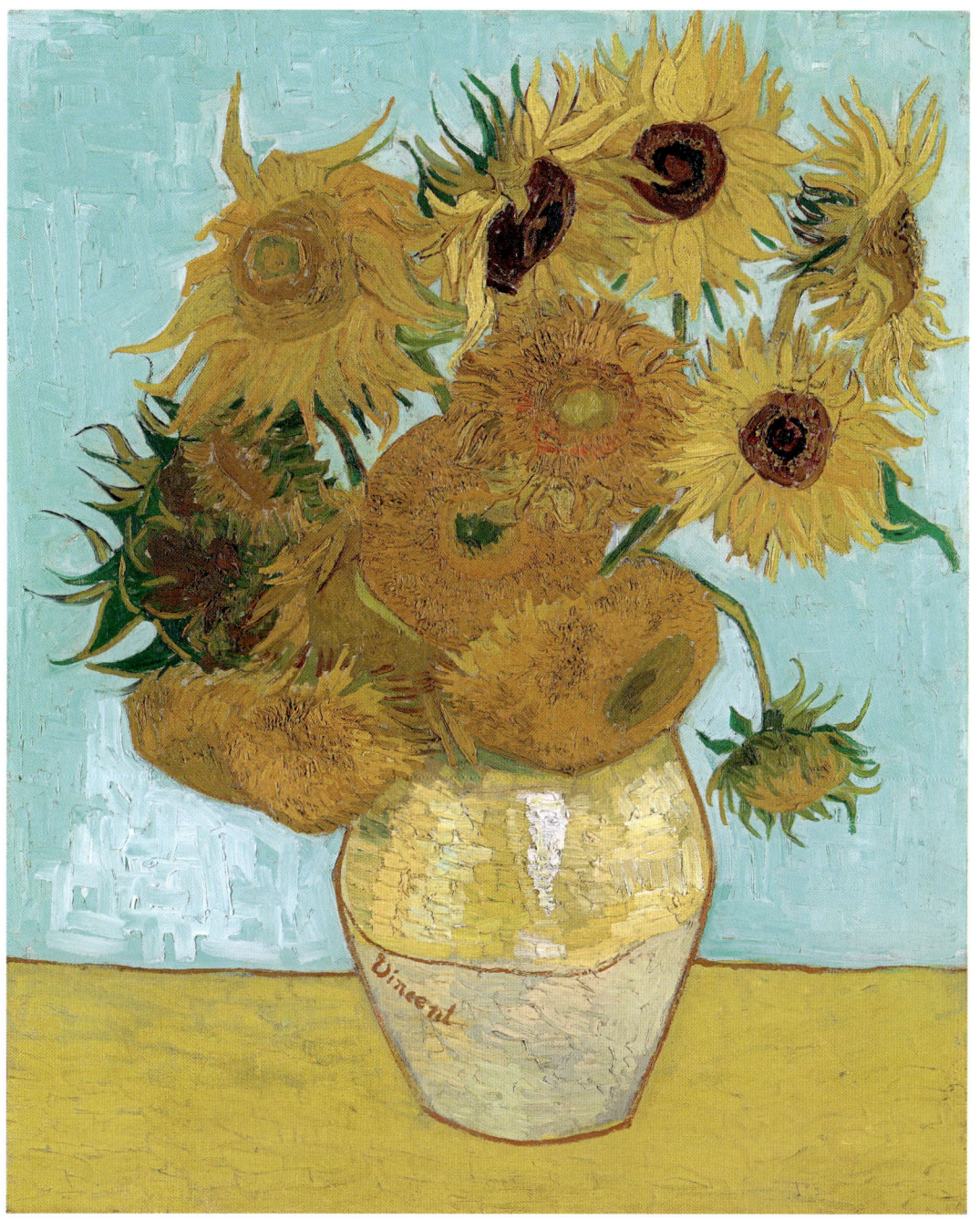

Terrace of a Café at Night, 1888

Oil on canvas
80.7 × 65.3 cm
Kröller-Müller Museum, Otterlo

The deep-blue sky with its many stars, the radiant yellow illuminated terrace—van Gogh's famous nighttime scene is a feast of colours. Black and grey are nowhere to be seen. He painted the café terrace on site, on the Place du Forum in the centre of Arles and was himself pleased with the effect he achieved with his choice of colours: the gaslight with its shades of yellow and orange would intensify the blue of the night, he wrote. Beneath the café's awning, lit by a gas lantern, he uses a warm yellow, orange and green. These tones do indeed contrast sharply with the picture's many shades of blue, from the greyish blue of the façades in the foreground to the starry night sky, to the dark blue of the more distant buildings.

Vincent wrote to his sister Wil why he liked painting on site at night: "It often strikes me that the night is even more richly coloured than daytime with these uncommonly strong violets and blues and greens. If you look closely, you'll see that certain stars are a lemon-yellow, others glow in pink, green, blue, forget-me-not colours. . . . It gives me great delight to paint the night outdoors. . . . Of course it can happen that in the darkness I confuse a blue with green or a bluish purple with a pinkish one."

The painter not only observed the colours precisely, but also the actual constellation of the stars in the sky. So precisely indeed that astronomical research later confirmed a quite precise dating for his creation of the night sky: he painted it the way it appeared in the night of the 16th or 17th of September. Yet his prime interest was not in a scientifically accurate representation of such constellations, but in his pictures' effect.

Terrace of a Café at Night is one of van Gogh's most famous paintings. The Kröller-Müller collecting couple purchased it and more than seventy of the artist's other works. In doing so they amassed the world's second-largest van Gogh collection. Only in Amsterdam's Van Gogh Museum is there a larger selection to admire.

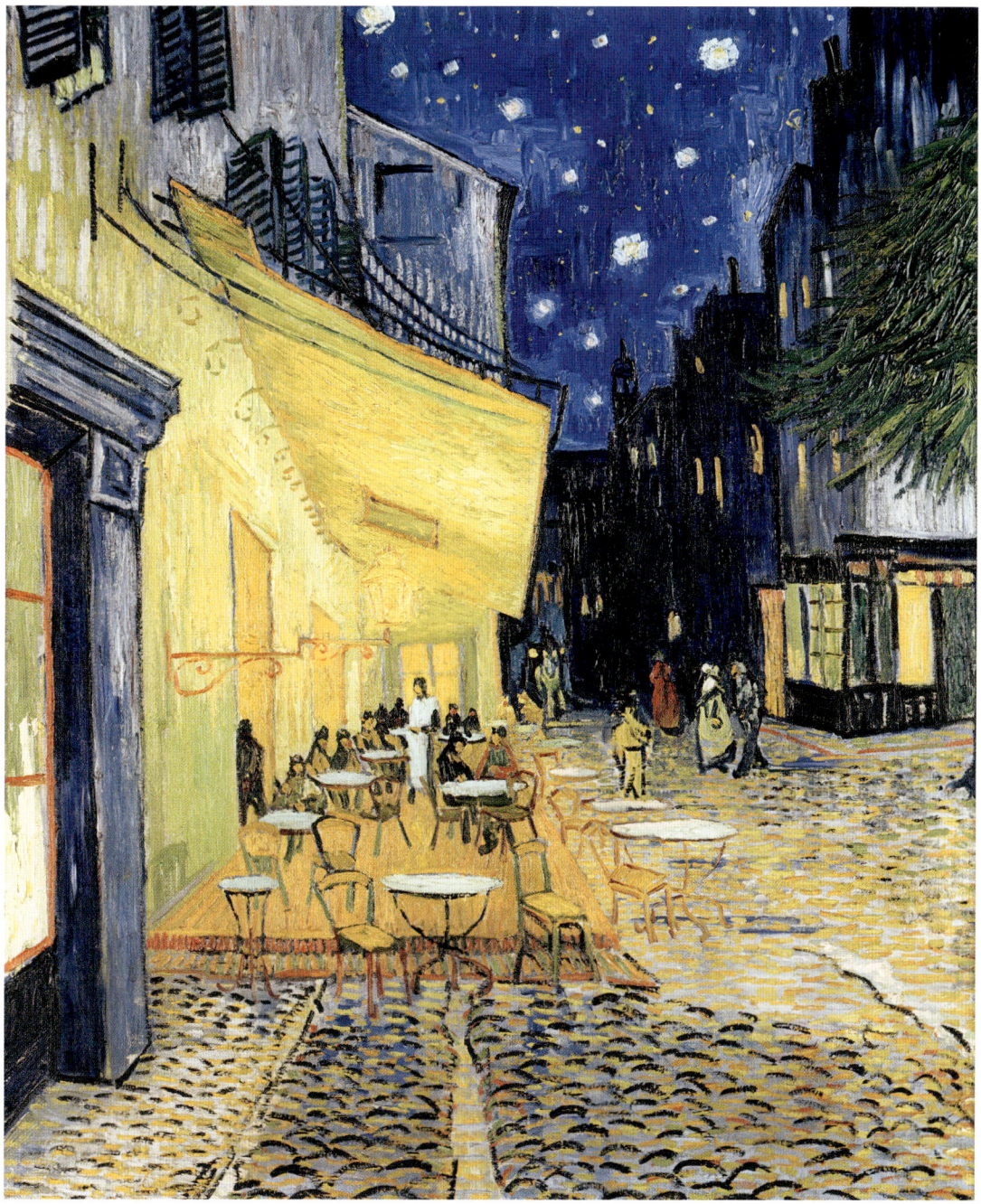

The Bedroom, 1888

Oil on canvas
72.4 × 91.3 cm
Van Gogh Museum, Amsterdam

Van Gogh repeatedly painted his Yellow House in the centre of Arles, happy in his new home and atelier. In October he described his newest picture to Theo: "This time it's quite simply my bedroom. Colour alone has to achieve the effect and with its simplification gives the objects a greater style and the overall suggestion of calm and of sleep." He then proceeded to describe the distribution of his colours in detail: "The walls are a light violet, the floor has red tiles, the wooden beds are as yellow as fresh butter, the curtain, the ceiling and the pillows are a lemon-yellow and green and very bright. The bedspreads are scarlet-red and the window green. The washstand is orange, the pitcher blue. The doors purple. And that's everything — there's nothing else in the room."

Comparing this description with the painting today, one discovers certain discrepancies. The colour contrasts appear to be considerably greater than van Gogh intended. Today the walls and doors in the Amsterdam painting are blue, no longer violet. The floor and the bed pillows are by no means the colours indicated in his letter—the work's colours are very different from those in Vincent's description. The same is also true of the two other pictures of his bedroom that van Gogh painted somewhat later, now in Paris's Musée d'Orsay and the Art Institute of Chicago.

How can it be that the pictures fail to conform to van Gogh's detailed description of them? Scholars have intensively studied all three works and determined that in the intervening decades they have faded considerably. The walls and doors were originally shades of violet, not blue and the floor looked different as well; it's red was more radiant than the one we see today. The colour reconstruction of the Amsterdam picture shows that the violet-reddish tone predominated, balancing out the contrasting yellow. This was how van Gogh produced the calming effect he intended: "The impression of the picture should calm the mind, or rather the imagination."

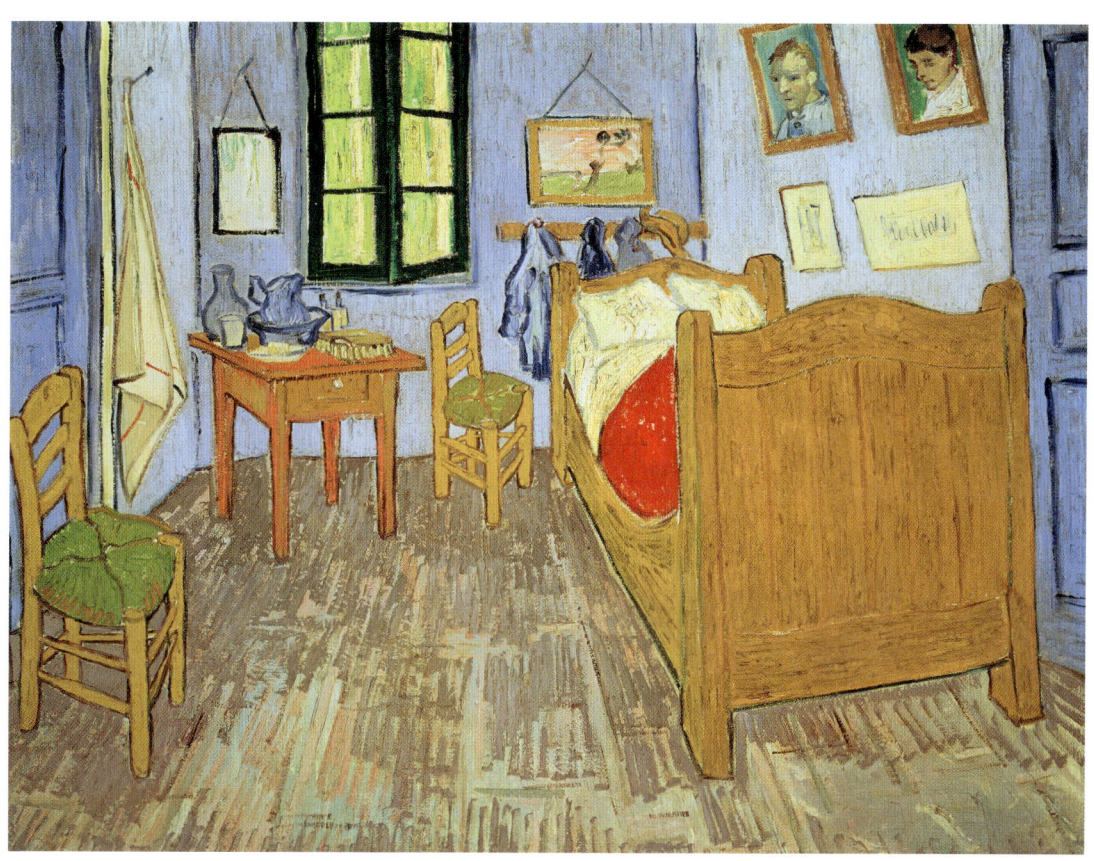

The Red Vineyard, 1888

Oil on canvas
75 × 93 cm
The Pushkin Museum of Fine Arts, Moscow

Among the many myths associated with Vincent van Gogh is the assertion that he managed to sell only a single painting during his lifetime. The number of works sold by the painter himself or by Theo at his behest may have been small, but it was certainly more than one. While the artist was painting canvas after canvas in Arles and sending them to Theo, people in Paris began to take notice of his work, not only other artists but also critics. He began to receive invitations to take part in exhibitions, but each time Vincent hesitated, pondering the pros and cons and Theo went along with him: "I feel that we can patiently wait until success comes, you will surely live to see it."

Theo was wrong, success was not forthcoming. Vincent's work was seen in Brussels in 1889 at an exhibition by the artists' group Les Vingt; after the two brothers had consulted, Theo submitted six of Vincent's paintings. One was this landscape with a red vineyard that Vincent had painted in Provence. In November 1888 he wrote to his brother about a joint painting outing with Gauguin: "But Monday, if only you had been with us! We saw a red, completely red vineyard, like red wine. In the distance it turned yellow, then there was a grey sky with sun above it. The ground was violet after the rain and shimmered yellow in the spots where the setting sun was reflected in it." At the Les Vingt exhibition the picture was purchased by the painter Anna Boch. The letter in which Theo reported the sale has not survived, but his younger brother entered the sum of 400 francs into his account books. He received the money on 6 March 1890 and it probably seemed like a decent enough price at the time.

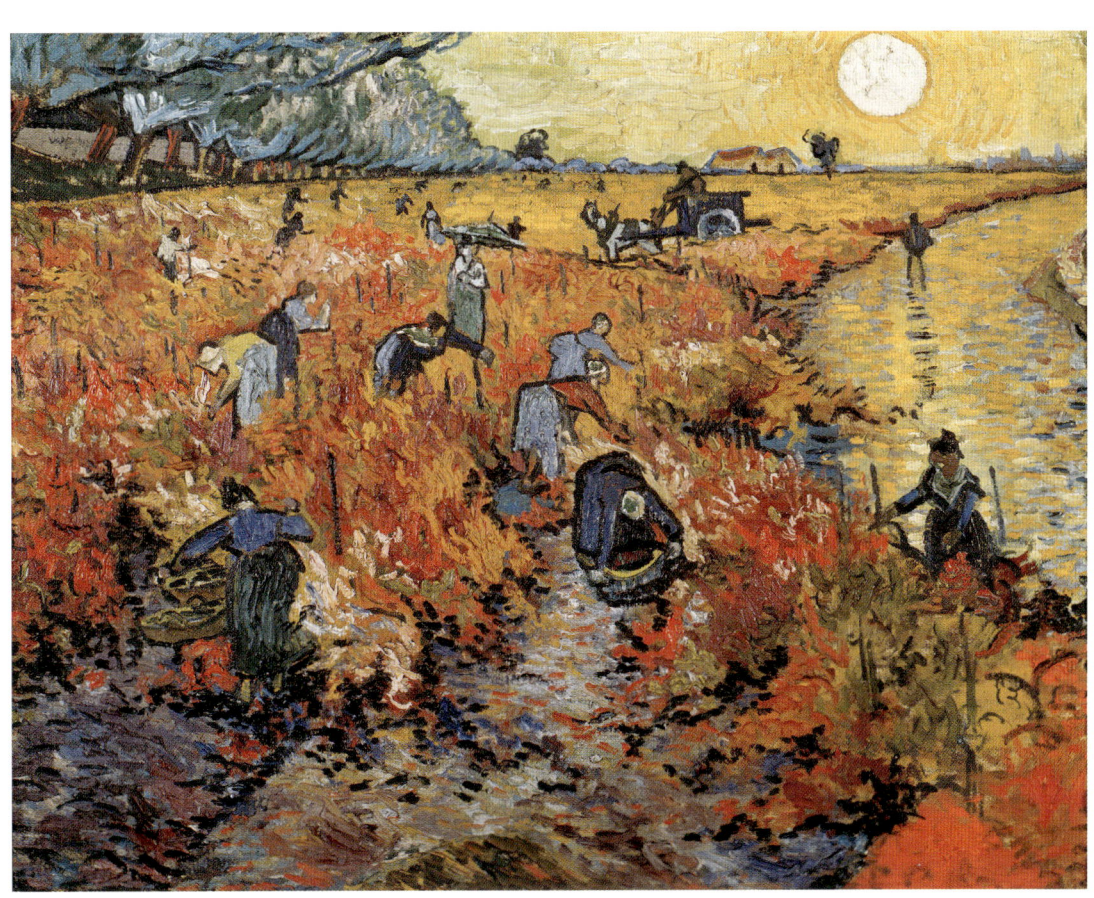

The Sower, 1888

Oil on canvas
32.5 × 40.3 cm
Van Gogh Museum, Amsterdam

Even before van Gogh thought of himself as an artist, or rather before he even began to draw, he avidly studied the works of Jean-François Millet. The French artist had unsparingly pictured the everyday lives of peasants in large paintings—and with them antagonised the public. Millet's name appears in Vincent's letters nearly 200 times, through all eighteen years of his correspondence. Vincent also adopted a motto of his: "dans l'art il faut y mettre sa peau". Sacrificing all of one's life for art, never sparing oneself or holding back; this accorded with Vincent's self-image from the start. Following his role model Millet, he considered himself a labourer among labourers.

The sower theme also goes back to the Frenchman. Van Gogh took up the motif again and again: his earliest engagement with it was as early as 1881, in the form of a copy after Millet and even a few months before his death the great master's motif still had a grip on him. Altogether, he drew and painted a sower in more than thirty of his works. The subject still attracted him in Arles, so in November 1888 he painted this picture. For several weeks that autumn he worked alongside the painter Paul Gauguin, who was then staying with him in Provence. Gauguin had urged him to rely more on his imagination in his pictures and less on reality. Accordingly, the sower here strides across his field like a saint, a radiant yellow sun painted with strong brush strokes frames his head like a halo. Beneath a greenish yellow sky blue fields extend back to the houses in the distance. In early December he wrote to his brother that it was already cold even in Arles. All the more reason for him to take up Gauguin's suggestion that he use his imagination—at least that meant he did not have to paint outside in the cold.

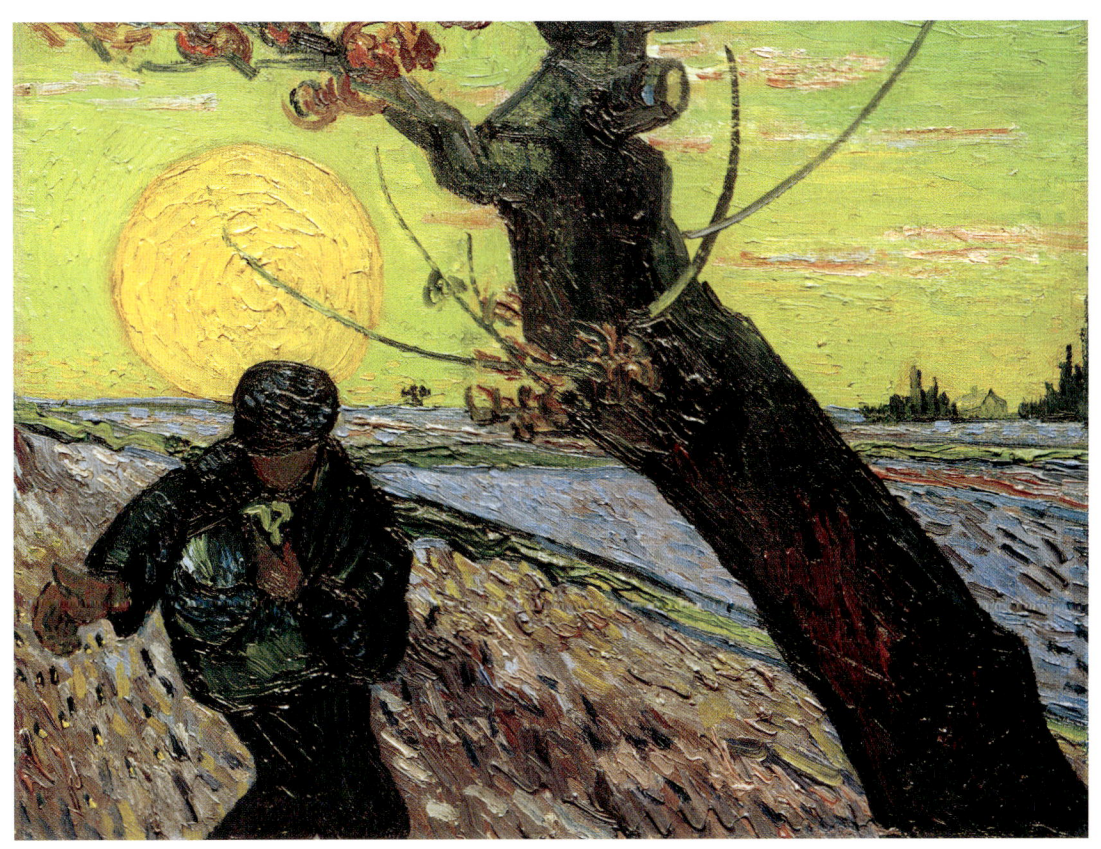

Portrait of Armand Roulin, 1888

Oil on canvas
65 × 54.1 cm
Museum Folkwang, Essen

What mattered most to van Gogh all his life was figure painting. He considered it his true artistic calling and it was the goal toward which he worked for years. Soon his greatest challenge was not the painting itself but finding models. In no case did he manage to do so. In his beginnings in Catholic Nuenen the churchmen forbade the local peasants from modelling for Vincent—they were even paid for turning down his requests. When the painter finally executed his first large figural picture, *The Potato Eaters* (page 48), a virtual avalanche of libel and slander was triggered when the maid van Gogh had portrayed in it became pregnant. The storm abated, but the painter's complaint about the absence of models for figure painting persisted. When he did manage to work with actual artists' models it was expensive, then "my portfolios expand to the degree that my purse shrinks".

The artist found it difficult to find models and pursue his passion for figure painting in Provence as well. But then quite unexpectedly he had an opportunity to portray several people of different ages. During his first summer in Arles he befriended the postmaster Joseph Roulin, who lived nearby. In July he arranged to paint a portrait of his new friend. And to his great delight the entire Roulin family modelled for him in the following months. In the winter van Gogh painted a number of portraits of family members, from the bearded letter carrier and his wife Augustine to the newborn daughter Marcelle. He painted two portraits of Roulin's oldest son Armand, one of them the picture from Essen's Museum Folkwang. The seventeen-year-old Armand is turned toward the viewer but gazes out of the picture. He wears a dark hat and a bright yellow jacket that stands out against a Veronese green background.

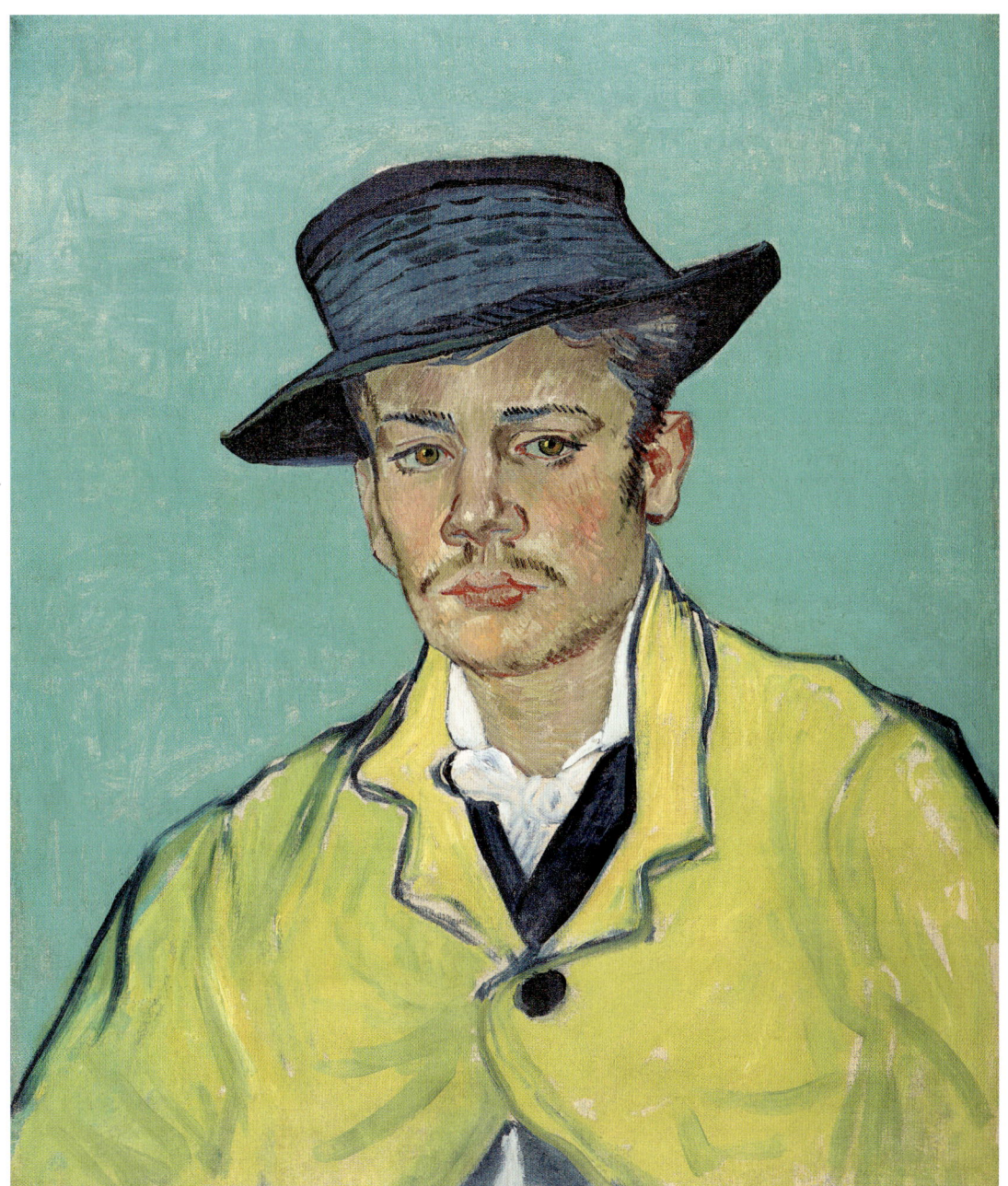

Still Life with a Plate of Onions, 1889

Oil on canvas
49.5 × 64.4 cm
Kröller-Müller Museum, Otterlo

Van Gogh was as compulsive about reading as he was about painting and writing letters—he indulged in it to extremes. He often kept his head above water by reading for weeks at a time. He immersed himself in the Bible over many years and later, with equal dedication, worked his way through the novels of the French naturalists Zola, Maupassant and Goncourt; devouring them all and eagerly discussing them with Theo: "Books, reality and art are one and the same to me." But whereas in early still lifes portraying books Zola's novel *La joie de vivre* is prominently placed or Maupassant's *Bel Ami*, in *Still Life with a Plate of Onions* the book visible on the table is a health manual. Its title is clearly *Annuaire de la Santé*, a book about good nutrition and hygiene that was popular in France at the time. Why did van Gogh place the book in the centre of his picture?

The artist had long been aware of what he was doing to himself with his painting, he saw himself falling apart. After a major breakdown he spent the turn of the year 1888/89 in the hospital in Arles. In early January he returned home—and immediately thought about the first pictures he would like to paint. He wrote to Theo that he wanted to begin with still lifes in order to reaccustom himself to painting. He reflected his return to the Yellow House in the everyday objects he collected on the wooden table: a plate with onions, the inevitable pipe and tobacco and letter from Theo, the empty wine bottle, the pot of coffee, the candle burning in a blue candlestick. And in the medical almanac with which he possibly hoped to calm himself as well as the one who would ultimately receive the picture: Theo. While still in hospital he had given his brother clear instructions: "Now I beg only a single thing from you, that you not upset yourself, for that upsets me too much in turn."

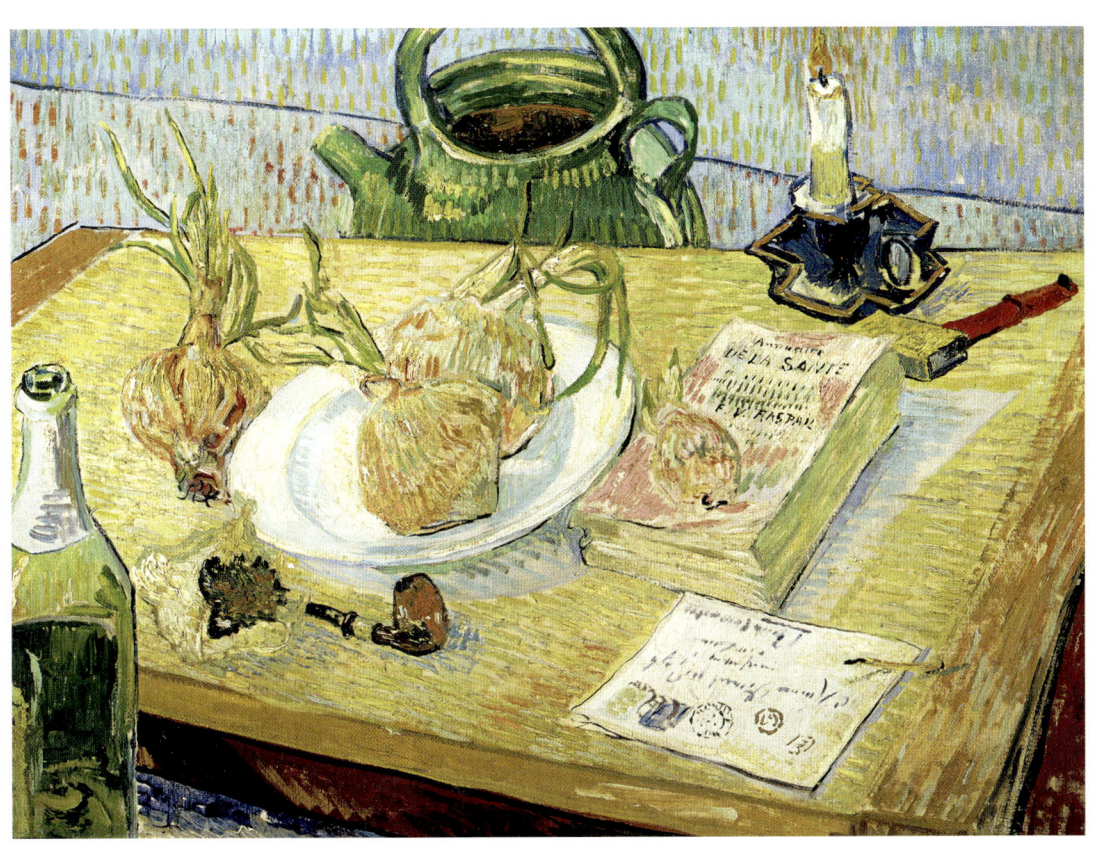

Self-Portrait with Bandaged Ear, 1889

Oil on canvas
60 × 49 cm
The Courtauld Gallery, London

Van Gogh painted this self-portrait in January 1889, after returning to his atelier in Arles. He had been released from hospital only a week before, the bandage still covering his ear. It was a self-inflicted wound; with his desperate act his dream of an artists' collaborative in Provence had ended. Paul Gauguin in particular was supposed to live with him in his 'southern atelier' in the Yellow House in Arles. And in the autumn of 1888 Gauguin had actually arrived and their weeks together were a productive period for both painters. Yet their so very different temperaments did not harmonise well. In December Vincent was certain that Gauguin would either leave soon and all of a sudden or else stay in Arles forever.

On 23 December things finally culminated in this "minor matter", as Vincent tried later to play it down: after a quarrel Gauguin left their shared atelier and Vincent cut off a portion of his left earlobe with a razor then carried it to a prostitute in town. After he returned to the Yellow House he was found there by a policeman who had been summoned and van Gogh was taken to hospital. By the time he was released Gauguin had already left. At the beginning of the year 1889 Vincent's dream of an artists' colony lay in pieces and he spent the following months in constant fear of new breakdowns. Nevertheless, immediately on returning home he painted himself: *Self-Portrait with Bandaged Ear* attests to his determination to keep painting even under difficult circumstances. His head is turned slightly to the side, so that our gaze falls on the large bandage covering his mutilated ear. With a fur-lined cap and thick jacket he has armed himself against the winter cold. One of the Japanese prints that he had long been collecting and that constantly inspired him hangs on the wall behind. A picture just begun stands on his easel—the painter has returned to his atelier. With strong brush strokes and a palette of bright colours Vincent van Gogh immortalises himself here on canvas.

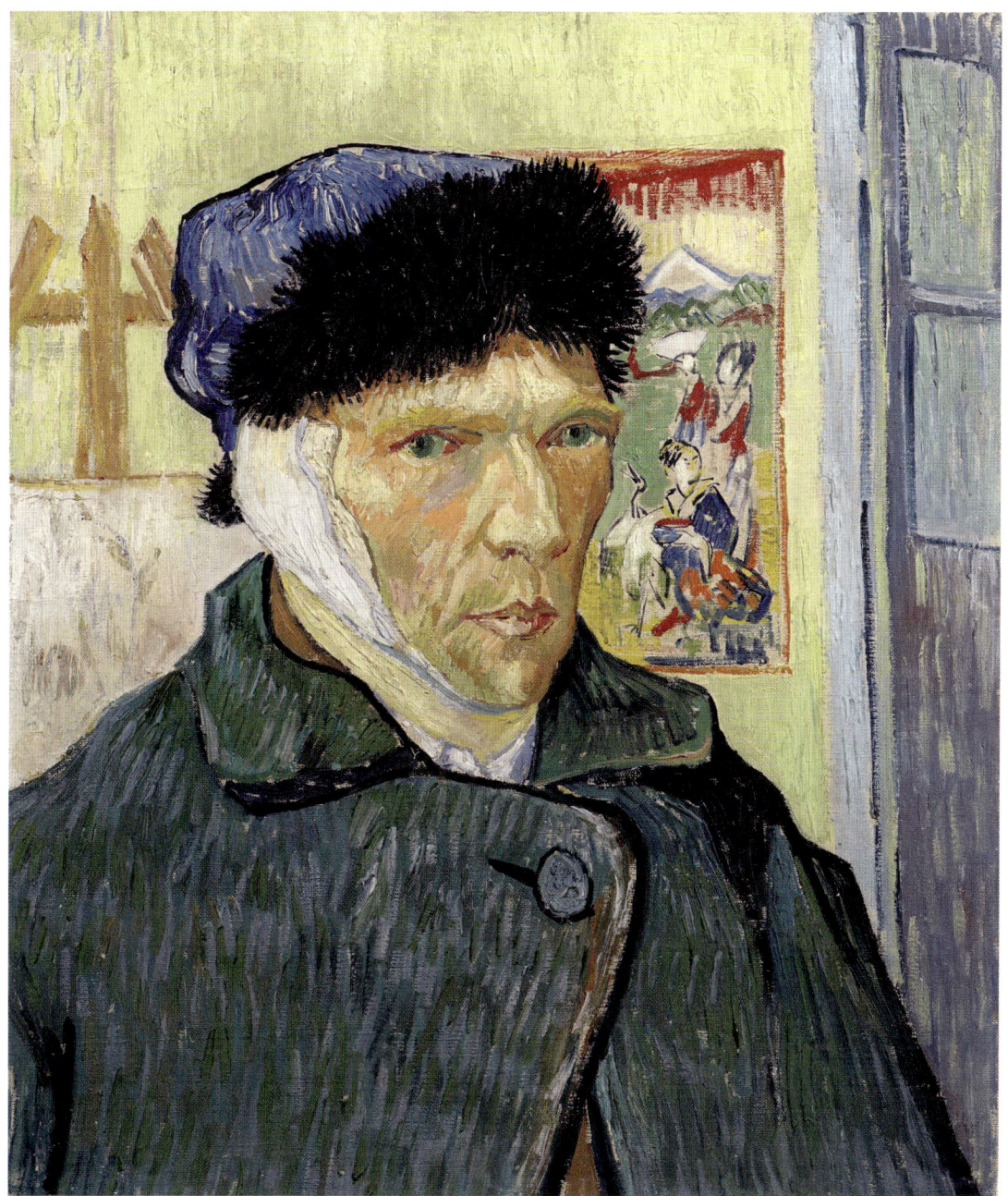

The Courtyard of the Hospital at Arles, 1889

Oil on canvas
73 × 92 cm
Sammlung Oskar Reinhart am Römerholz, Winterthur

After his psychotic attack in December 1888 van Gogh was taken to the hospital in
Arles but returned to his atelier in early January 1889. There he got back to work
immediately, painting still lifes and two self-portraits. But his return to the easel was
only of brief duration, his health was still volatile. After only a month in his atelier it
became clear that he was far from recovery. He was once again taken to the hospital
and again returned home. In the meantime his neighbours had become upset; they
petitioned the mayor against his return and the hostile mood in the town distressed
him. Already in late February he was re-admitted to the hospital again and this time
he stayed there for several weeks. But he was able to work again: he painted the
hospital courtyard with its colourful flowers, also the ward in which he was housed.

By this time van Gogh was convinced that the therapy provided in Arles was not
enough to cure him. What he had long been considering must have struck Theo
like a bolt from the blue: Vincent wanted to be in a mental institution. He explained
his decision to his brother before committing himself to the asylum at Saint-Rémy:
"Forgive me for not going into the details and explaining the plusses and minuses
of such a relocation. Talking about it would shatter my skull at the moment. I hope
it is enough to say that I feel wholly incapable of renting a new atelier and living
there alone, here or anywhere else, it matters not. I have tried to imagine starting
over again, but for the moment it is impossible. I fear losing the ability to return
to work if I were to overextend myself and had moreover saddled myself with all
the responsibility of an atelier. Temporarily I would like to be interned, for my own
peace of mind and also that of others."

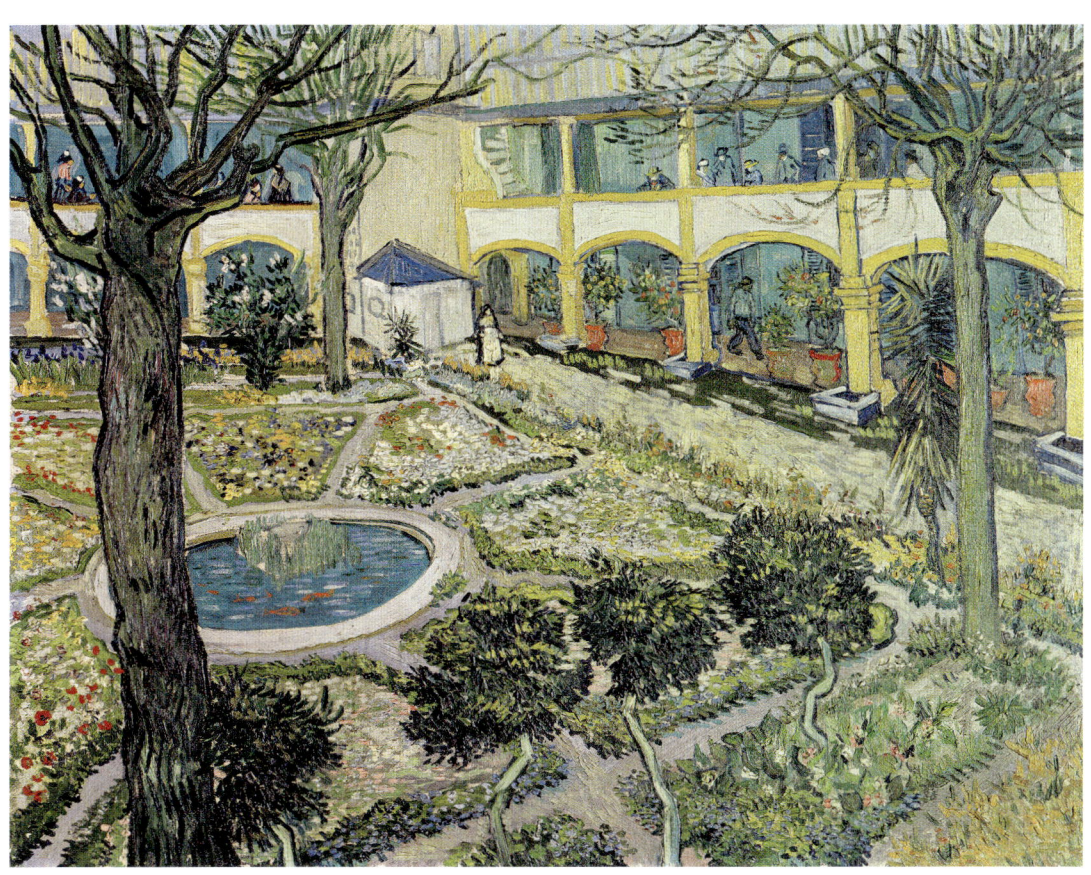

Irises, 1889

Oil on canvas
71 × 93 cm
The J. Paul Getty Museum, Los Angeles

Van Gogh painted these radiant blue irises rising up out of reddish soil at close range. The flowers fill the entire height of the canvas and are cut off by the picture's edge. Each plant is portrayed differently but with their animated blooms and leaves they constitute a waving sea of flowers. He called even this picture painted during his first weeks in Saint-Rémy a mere study. Yet he sent the work to Theo, as he did so with the majority of his works. When Theo received the canvas he was impressed. He submitted it to the Paris Salon des Indépendants and when the exhibition took place in September 1889, he enthusiastically wrote to his brother that his flower painting stood out even from a distance: "It is a beautiful study of air and life." In 1892 the work was purchased from Julien Tanguy by the French journalist and art critic Octave Mirbeau. Two years before, while the artist was still alive, Mirbeau had written an article praising Vincent's work in the most effusive terms.

The critic was not van Gogh's only admirer; the artist was gradually becoming better known. At the time of his death the majority of his works were in Paris in the care of his brother Theo, who had supported him throughout the years. When Theo died only months later the enormous collection of Vincent's pictures was inherited by Theo's wife. Johanna van Gogh-Bonger subsequently devoted herself to the promotion of Vincent's art: she lent his works to exhibitions and gallerists and so, after the turn of the century, the artist was known to a broader public. A first major show of his pictures (including the *Irises*) took place in Paris in 1901 and exhibitions in Amsterdam and Berlin were to follow. In 1914 Johanna van Gogh-Bonger published the correspondence between her brother-in-law and her husband. Art collectors were not alone in discovering van Gogh's painting: the early-twentieth-century Expressionists' highly emotional, bold application of colour was inspired by van Gogh's works from the last years of his life.

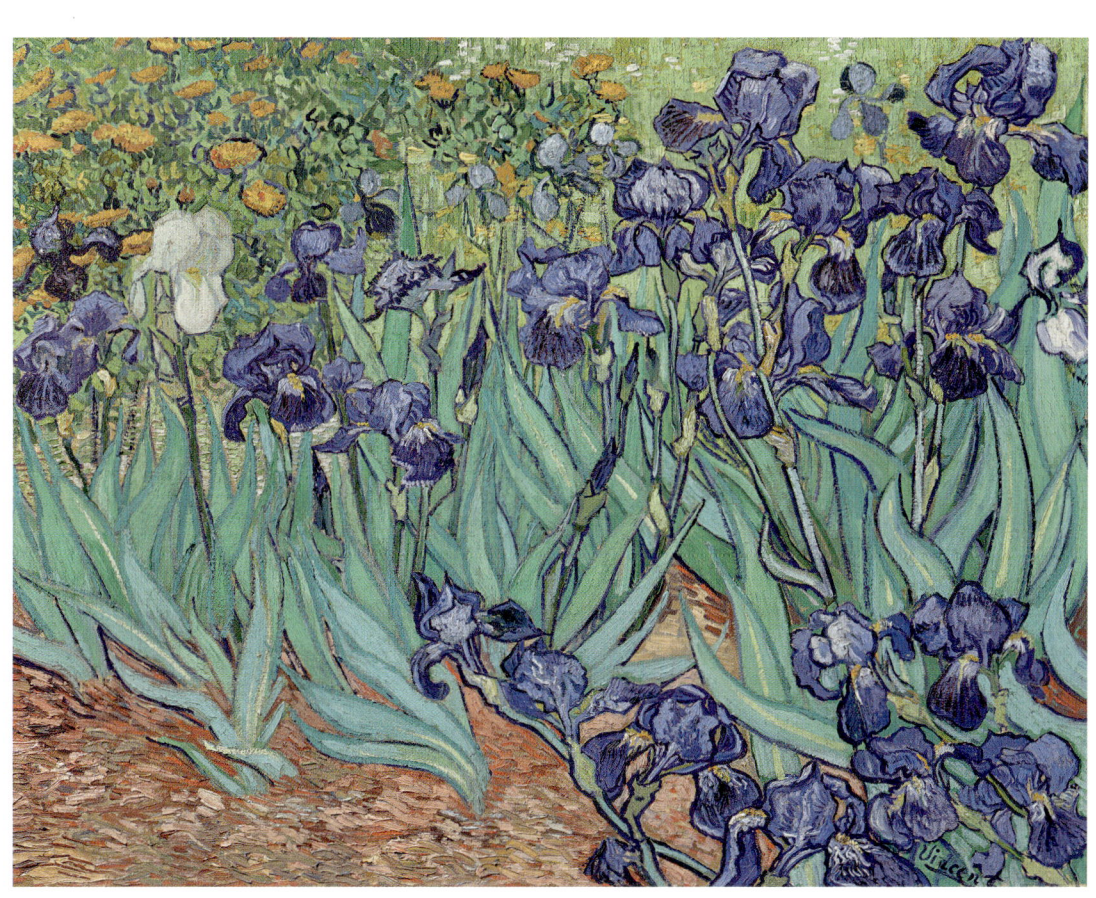

The Starry Night, 1889

Oil on canvas
73.7 × 92.1 cm
The Museum of Modern Art, New York

Vincent van Gogh's *The Starry Night* is one of the many highlights of New York's Museum of Modern Art. The painting pictures the sky over Saint-Rémy in the early morning of 18 June 1889. Researchers have discovered that the date can be determined from the position of the stars. The nighttime landscape seems dreamy and turbulent, radiant stars whirl across a sky full of motion as the moon lends a warm glow to the scene.

Despite the precise observation behind all this—the work was not painted outdoors. In Provence Van Gogh had taken to painting outdoors at night and reported in detail on other pictures he had produced that way. But in June 1889 his circumstances had changed; fear of suffering further psychotic episodes had made his life unbearable, so he had committed himself to the mental home in Saint-Rémy-de-Provence the previous month. Associating with the other patients made him anxious and painting became all-important to him. He first portrayed what he could see through the barred window of his room. Here he blended his observations of the night sky with invented elements: the large cypress, for example, the pointed church tower between the town's small houses—none of this could be seen from his window. Perhaps he recalled these features from previous studies. In November of the previous year, while painting together with his artist colleague Gauguin, he had written to his brother: "Now I often work from my imagination. Such pictures are always less inept and look more artificial than studies done directly from nature." The large bright star just to the right of the cypress, however, was observed by van Gogh quite precisely; the planet Venus was indeed a luminous spot in the sky that summer.

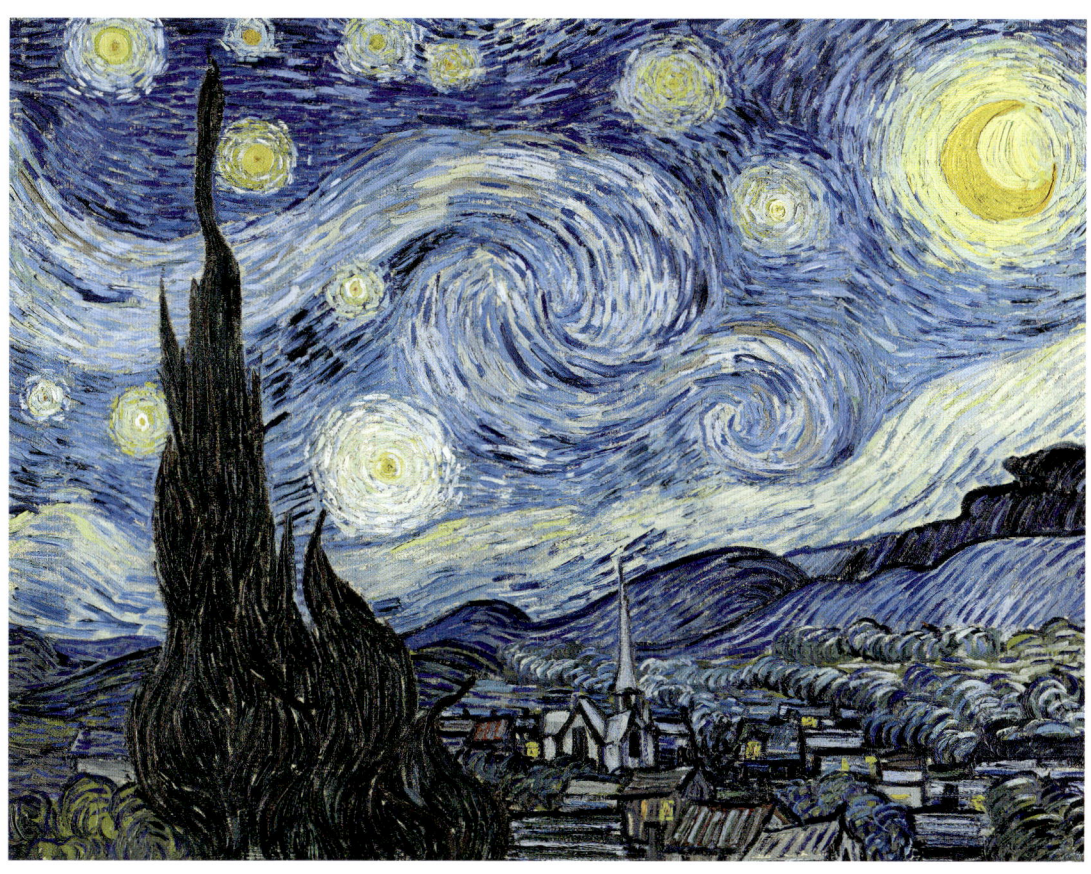

Wheat Field with Cypresses, 1889

Oil on canvas
73 × 93.4 cm
The Metropolitan Museum of Art, New York

A golden field of wheat surrounding a shimmering young olive tree, tall, dark-green cypresses, hazy bluish mountains in the background—this is van Gogh's Provence. Here it lies beneath swirls of clouds in blue, sea-green and white. In his letters van Gogh frequently complained about the mistral, the cold summer wind that prevails over southern France for days at a time and which made painting outdoors nearly impossible. Here the wind appears to animate the entire landscape; everything whirls in powerful rhythmic lines and bold brush strokes.

Like *The Starry Night* (page 94), this picture was painted while van Gogh was staying in the mental asylum in Saint-Rémy. If accompanied by an orderly he was allowed to leave the grounds and work nearby, where he produced the first version of *Wheat Field with Cypresses*. The artist devoted a whole series of paintings to the Provençal landscape with its characteristic cypress trees. At the end of June he wrote to Theo: "The cypresses are still keeping me busy, I would gladly make something with them comparable to the sunflower pictures, for it astonishes me that no one has painted them the way I see them." How van Gogh saw them changed during the time he spent in the south of France. In Saint-Rémy he was wholly captivated by the trees and further explained to Theo how sublime they seemed to him: "...beautiful with respect to lines and proportions like an Egyptian obelisk. And their green has such a refined quality. It is the dark spot in a sun-filled landscape". He also considered *Wheat Field with Cypresses* only a study: after this he produced a pen drawing and two more oil paintings featuring the same motif, one of which he wanted to give to his mother and sister. To his thinking it was one of his best paintings from this summer.

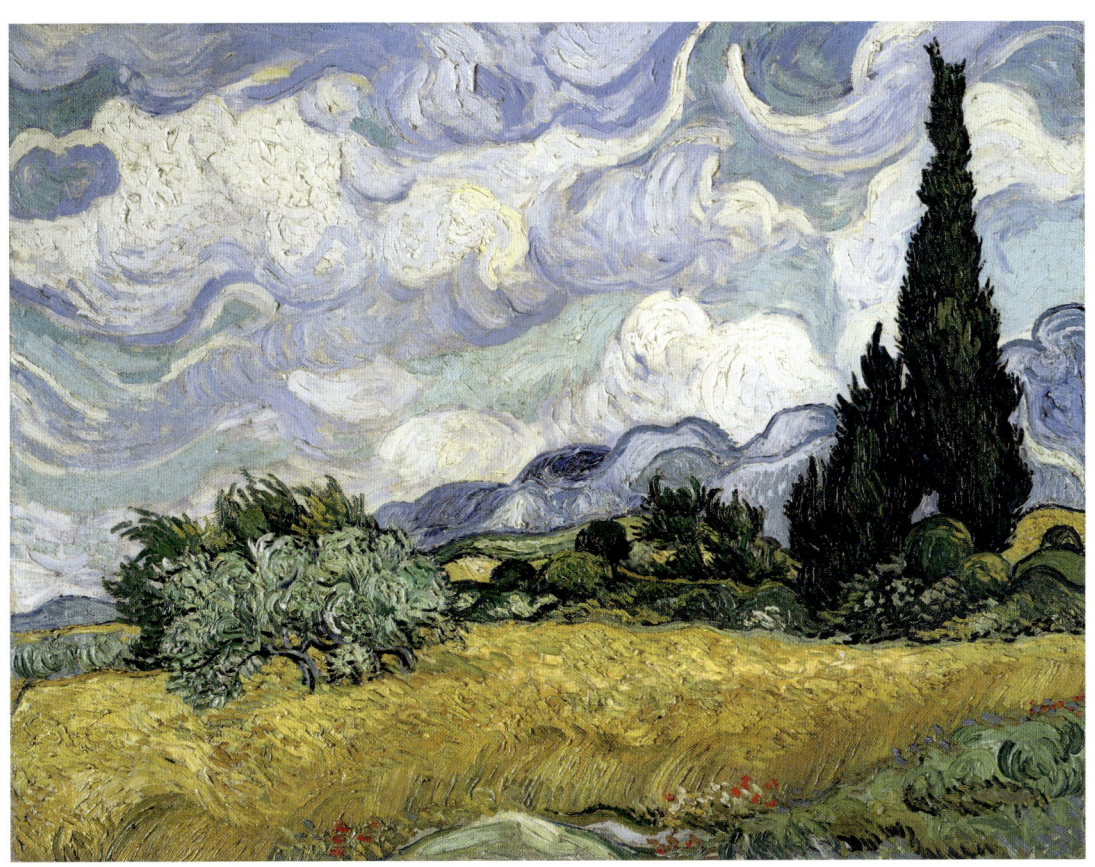

Olive Grove, 1889

Oil on canvas
72.4 × 91.9 cm
Kröller-Müller Museum, Otterlo

Van Gogh preferred painting outdoors. Many of his pictures were made quickly and directly in front of his motif, whether in the Dutch moorland or under the Provençal sun. He was not alone, many nineteenth-century painters liked to work outside instead of in their ateliers, most notably the Impressionists. After the middle of the century, when oil pigments became available in tubes and art supply shops sold pre-grounded canvas, painting outdoors had become simpler, though it was still somewhat more troublesome than indoor work. In several letters van Gogh described the challenges of working outside. Once after painting some farmhouses he complained to Theo: "Just head outside sometime and set yourself down and paint on site! Then anything can happen—out of the four pictures you will receive I picked out a hundred flies or more, not to mention the dust and sand etc., and also not to mention that if you carry them through heath and hedges for a couple of hours one or another twig scratches them etc. Once you get to the open fields after a couple of hours' march in this weather you're tired and hot; the figures don't stand still like professional models and the conditions change over the course of the day."

In another passage van Gogh describes how on one occasion he was unable to bring his completed pictures back with him from his painting outing: the oil pigments were still too wet. That nature occasionally left its physical traces in his pictures is attested by *Olive Grove* illustrated here. Van Gogh painted most of the picture on site, between olive trees outside the gates of the Saint-Rémy asylum: in the pigment are small traces of plants, grains of sand and even insect tracks. Restorers at New York's Metropolitan Museum have also discovered outdoor debris in his *Wheat Field with Cypresses* (page 96).

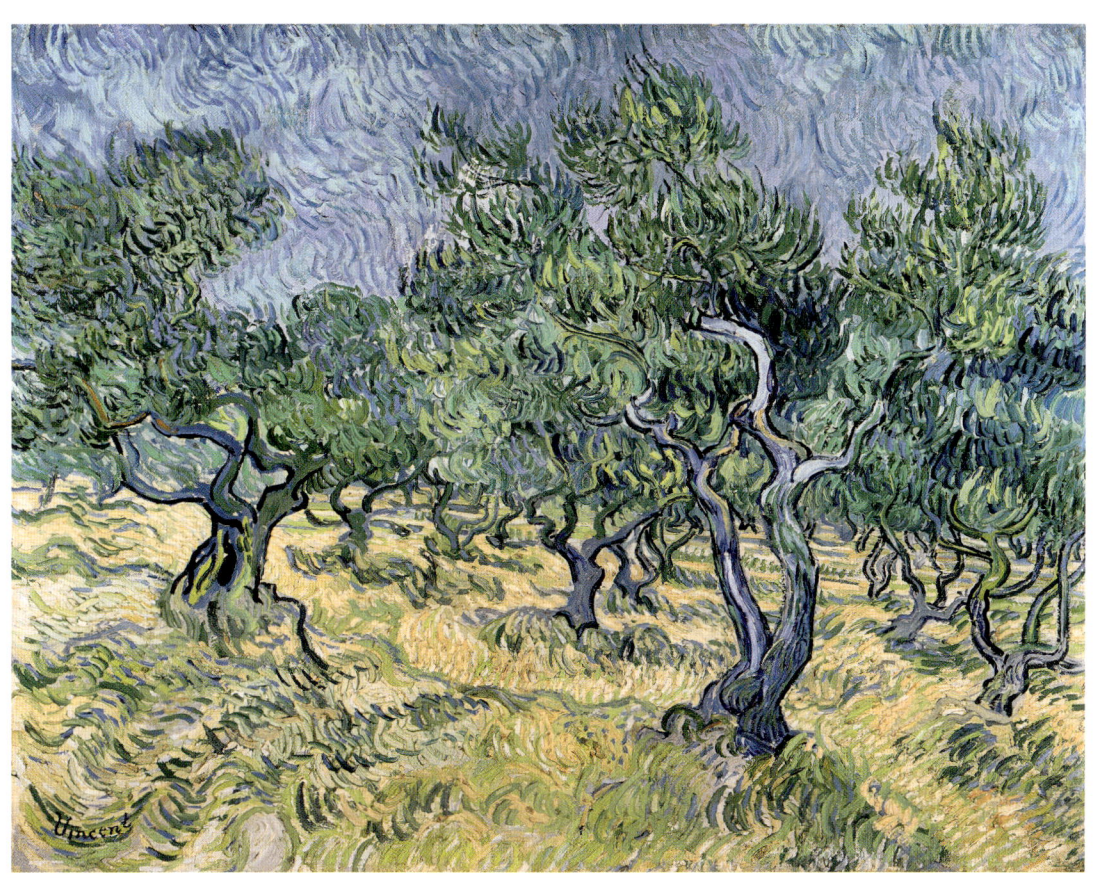

Self-Portrait, 1889

Oil on canvas
57.8 × 44.5 cm
National Gallery of Art, Washington

Van Gogh painted a full three dozen self-portraits. The Washington canvas, painted in the summer of 1889, is one of his last. Here he presents himself as an artist at work, wearing a blue smock and holding the palette with pigments and brushes in his hand. His smock and the background were painted in shades of blue applied in long brush strokes following the outline of his head. His pale, almost greenish face is framed by short hair in a light orange-blonde and a shaggy beard in a somewhat darker rust-orange. He is gazing questioningly, sceptically at the viewer out of the corners of his eyes.

Van Gogh painted this picture after several months stay in Saint-Rémy. When he first arrived at the asylum he painted only landscapes, like *Wheat Field with Cypresses* (page 96). But during a painting excursion into its surroundings he suffered another serious breakdown and for a full five weeks found himself incapable of working. The episode shattered him; unsure of himself, he withdrew, even refusing to enter the asylum's garden. He had barely found his strength again when, as a first trial, he painted this self-portrait—it is distinctly unsettling. In early September he wrote to his brother: "They say—and I am certainly prepared to believe it—that it is difficult to know yourself, but also it isn't easy to paint yourself. So at the moment I am working on two self-portraits—for want of another model—because it's high time that I work on figures a bit. One of them I began when I got back on my feet; I was thin and pale as a ghost. It is a dark violet-blue and the head whitish with yellow hair, so it has a colour effect." He also described the second self-portrait in which he is seen painting in front of a similarly animated but lighter background; it now hangs in Paris's Musée d'Orsay.

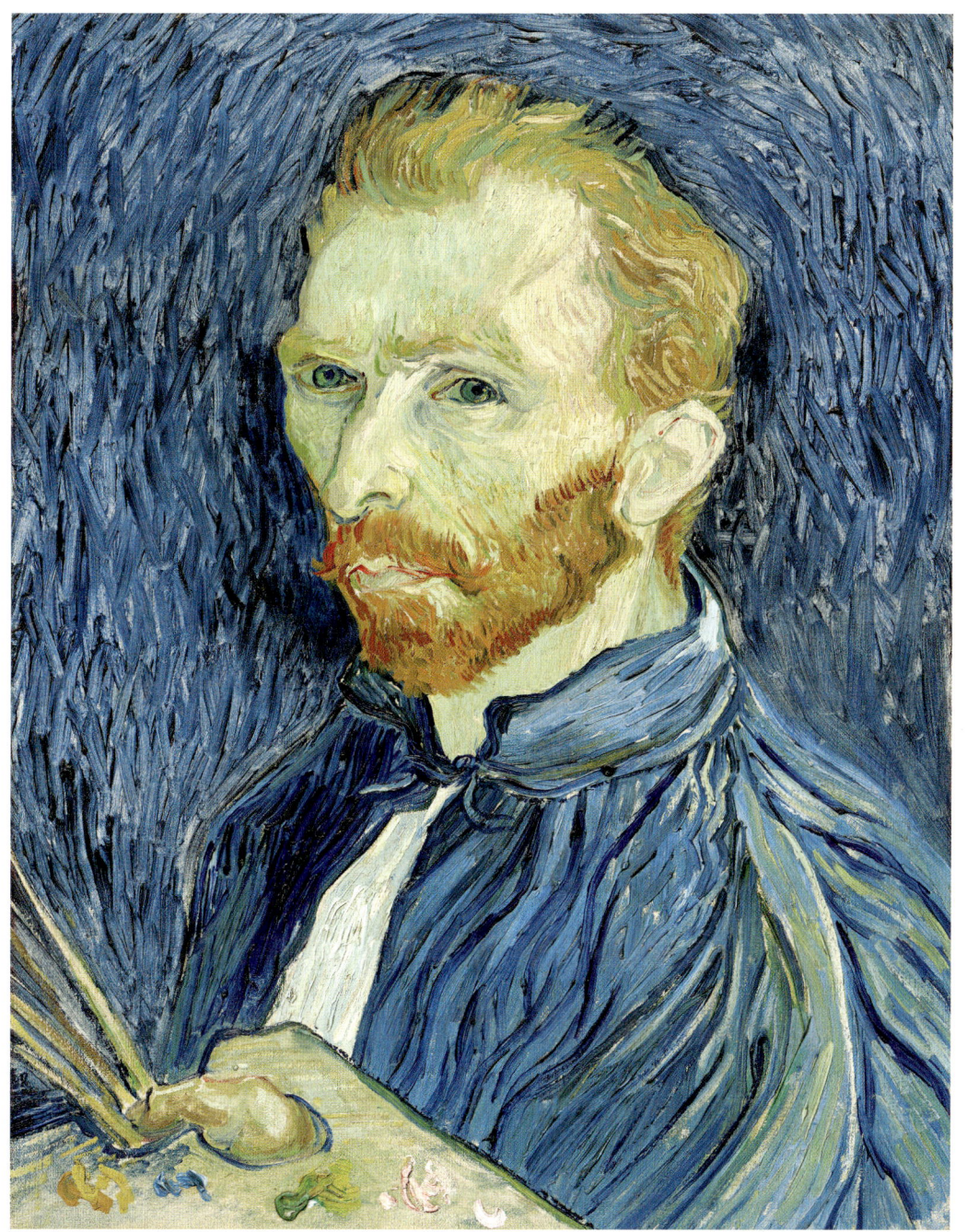

Almond Blossom, 1890

Oil on canvas
73.3 × 92.4 cm
Van Gogh Museum, Amsterdam

When Theo's wife Johanna gave birth to a son in early 1890 a letter was immediately sent to Vincent: "As we already wrote, we are going to name him after you and would wish that he might become as persevering and courageous as you are." Vincent would have preferred that the child be named after his father, but as he wrote to his mother in February 1890 that was his only objection: "But as always, since it has already happened, I immediately began to make a painting for him, to hang in their bedroom. Large branches with white almond blossoms in front of a blue sky."

Blooming branches in front of a blue spring sky were one of van Gogh's favourite motifs. But the perspective he chose here is unusual. He painted the branches from below and at close range, so we can't see the rest of the almond tree. Focusing on a single detail and cropping it closely was a compositional scheme the painter knew from Japanese colour prints. The motif itself and the strong contours also point to them as his inspiration.

In early 1890 the almond blossom marked a new beginning for van Gogh in two respects: he had now been living more than six months in the mental home Saint-Paul-de-Mausole. After a long artistic pause he had just begun to take up his paints and brushes again. When the picture for his nephew was finished he sent it to Theo and Johanna, who hung it in their living room. After the van Gogh brothers died, one after another, Johanna van Gogh-Bonger owned all of Vincent's paintings. In the next few years she sold some of her brother-in-law's works, but the blooming almond branches, the present to her son Vincent Willem, she kept with her always. It is hardly surprising that she and her son were especially fond of this painting. The younger Vincent Willem would later establish the Van Gogh Museum in Amsterdam, in which his almond branches hang today. The painting has lost some of its brilliance over the years. The buds and blossoms were distinctly pinkish originally, but owing to the influence of light they have bleached and are now whiter.

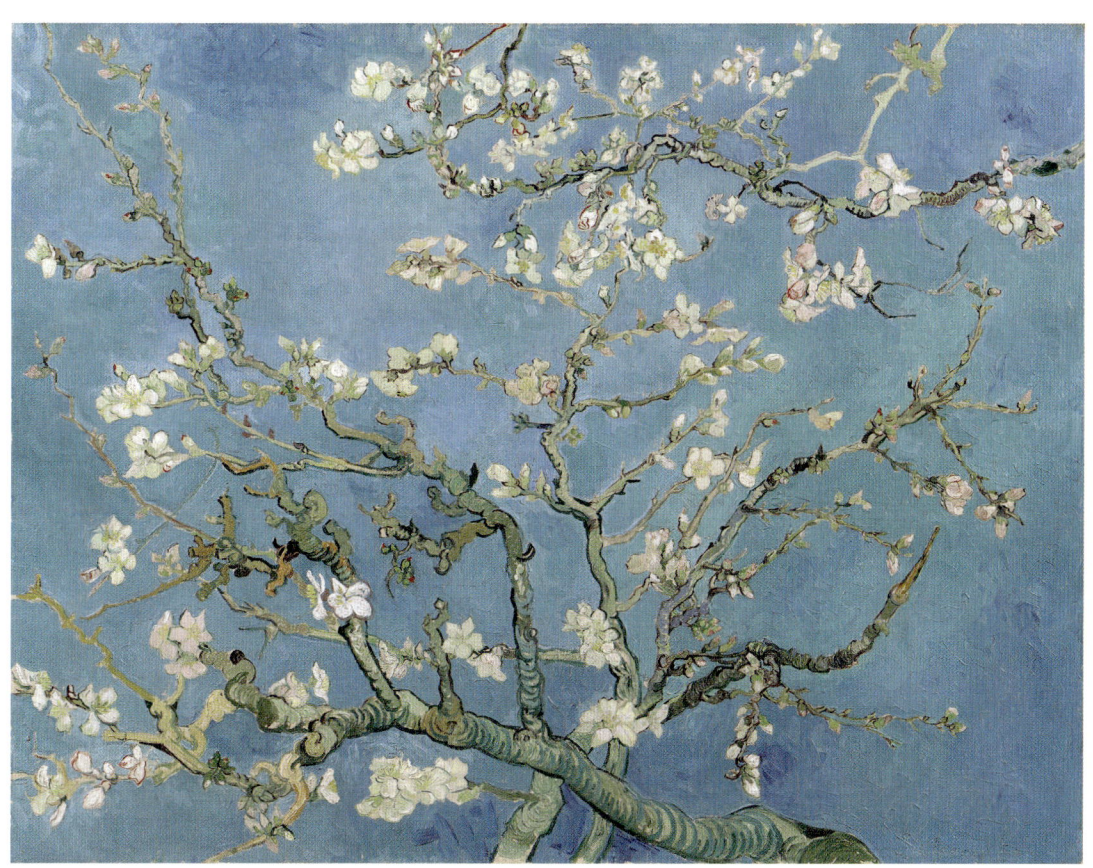

Portrait of Dr Gachet, 1890

Oil on canvas
67 × 56 cm
Whereabouts unknown

After more than two years in the south of France Vincent van Gogh moved in May 1890 to Auvers, a small town north of Paris, where he sought out the physician Dr Gachet. Theo had met Gachet through an artist friend and hoped that the doctor could help Vincent. Gachet enjoyed being in the company of artists and was interested in van Gogh's pictures. He prescribed a kind of working therapy: van Gogh painted picture after picture in Auvers—and twice portrayed Dr Gachet himself.

The doctor slumps in his chair, propped up on his right elbow on the table in front of him, with his head resting on his hand. Gachet's melancholy gaze extends into the distance. The picture relies on strong colour effects: the yellow-bound books contrast with the dark-blue jacket, the green leaves of the blooming foxglove stand out against the red table. The painting's surface is animated by bold brush strokes, yet Gachet's facial expression is calm, meditative. Van Gogh described to his sister Wil the effect he hoped for in portraits like this: "I WOULD LIKE, you see, but by no means maintain that I can manage it, although—I am trying in any case, I would like to make portraits that would strike people a century later as apparitions. For that reason I don't try to picture us with photographic accuracy but with evident emotions, employing as expressive means and for intensification of the personality our science and our modern taste in colours."

Much is known about the history of this portrait, there is even a whole book about it, yet the work has not been on public view for more than thirty years. Its itinerary runs as follows: the Städel Museum purchased the painting from a gallerist in 1911. The work remained in Frankfurt until the National Socialists confiscated it in 1937 and declared it degenerate. After the Second World War the painting was in a private collection. And precisely 100 years after van Gogh painted it the portrait was auctioned in New York. It fetched a price that seems unbelievable to this day: eighty-two million dollars. It was sold to the Japanese industrialist Ryoei Saito. Since that auction in 1990 the picture has never been exhibited. The second version of the portrait can nevertheless still be admired in a museum, it hangs in Paris's Musée d'Orsay.

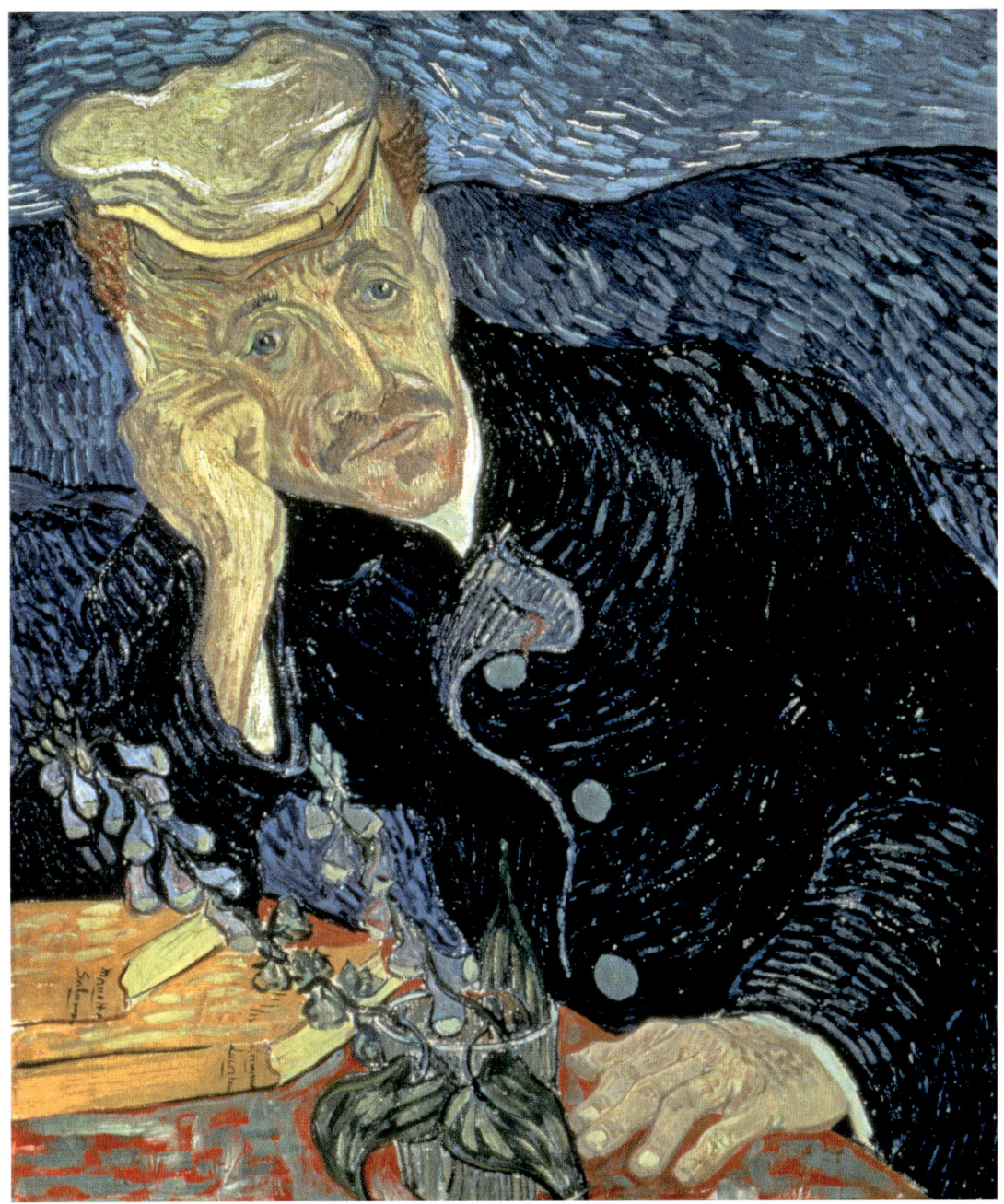

Plain near Auvers, 1890

Oil on canvas
73.5 × 92 cm
Neue Pinakothek, Munich

Van Gogh spent the last two months of his life in the north of France in Auvers-sur-Oise. The small town, reached from Paris by train, had already been a major inspiration for such painters as Daubigny, Corot, Cézanne and Gauguin, and it also kept van Gogh on his toes. He sped up his already impressive working tempo one last time. For each day he spent there he left behind a painting.

With its thatched cottages and handsome farmhouses Auvers lies in the midst of gentle hills and extensive wheat fields. The fields and small houses, the village church, one or another local he portrayed—all this provided subject matter for his pictures. One of the works created in these two months was the oil painting *Plain near Auvers*. Clouds composed of swirls of blue and white pigment are clustered in the sky, the fields in green ochre tones are rendered in straight brush strokes. The meadow in the foreground with its brush strokes in different directions seems wilder. Van Gogh produced two additional variants of this panorama. Like most of his works, he thought of them not as pictures but as studies—though they too, he insisted, have their value. Altogether, in the two months he spent in Auvers he produced roughly seventy pictures as well as thirty drawings. He was aware that he would be criticised for working so fast, but he could hardly hold back. To Theo, who was ultimately supposed to sell his brother's work, he argued convincingly: "I can already predict that everybody will find that I work too fast. Don't believe it. . . . If people tell you that it is painted too quickly you can respond by saying that they looked at it too quickly."

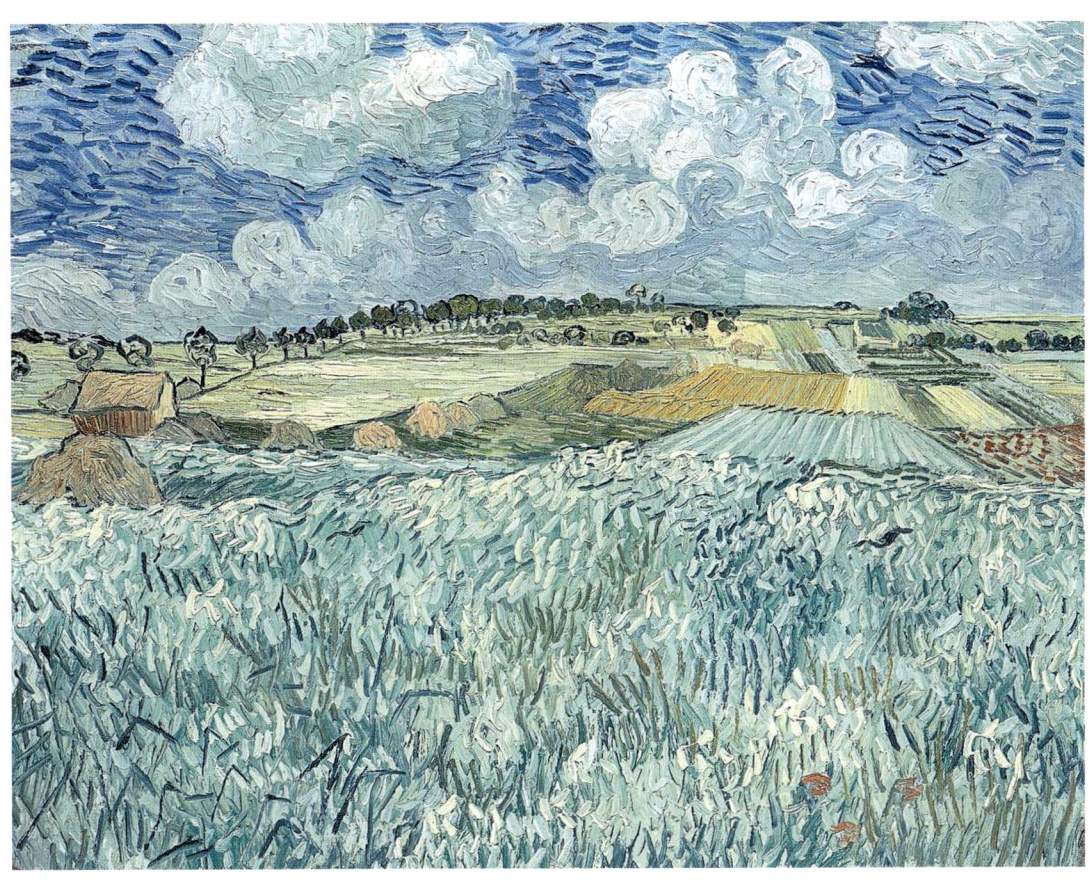

Daubigny's Garden, 1890

Oil on canvas
53.2 × 103.5 cm
Rudolf Staechelin Collection, Basel

The small town Auvers-sur-Oise north of Paris had already inspired a number of artists. The landscape painter Charles-François Daubigny, who van Gogh had admired his whole life, had also lived there. When van Gogh arrived in Auvers he visited the artist's garden and promptly captured it in paintings. He first devoted only a small canvas to the garden, more precisely a linen dishtowel, probably because he didn't happen to have anything else to paint on at hand. He later set about painting a larger version of the motif. This time he used an especially broad format like those of his role model Daubigny. The new painting was a full metre wide—room for a whole garden panorama. Vincent wrote to Theo in July that he considered this canvas one of his best. In his next-to-last letter he described the picture in detail, including a large drawing above his lines so that his brother could immediately picture the work. He described its colours in detail, from the "nut tree with violet leaves" to the pink house with bluish roof tiles to the black cat in the foreground.

Even in the last weeks of his life in Auvers, while painting around seventy pictures at an incredible rate, van Gogh expressed his ideas precisely and composed his paintings with care. Indeed although what may strike us as that summer's obsessive, uncontrollable slap-dash painting, van Gogh himself placed each picture within the context of his work and did his 'brain work', as he called it. His determination and clear view of his own achievement tend to be forgotten among the over-exaggerated legends about his life. Even at the beginning of his time in Provence, van Gogh realised what he was going to be undertaking: "Work now has me in its claws, probably forever, I feel, and though that's no misfortune, I envision fortune quite otherwise."

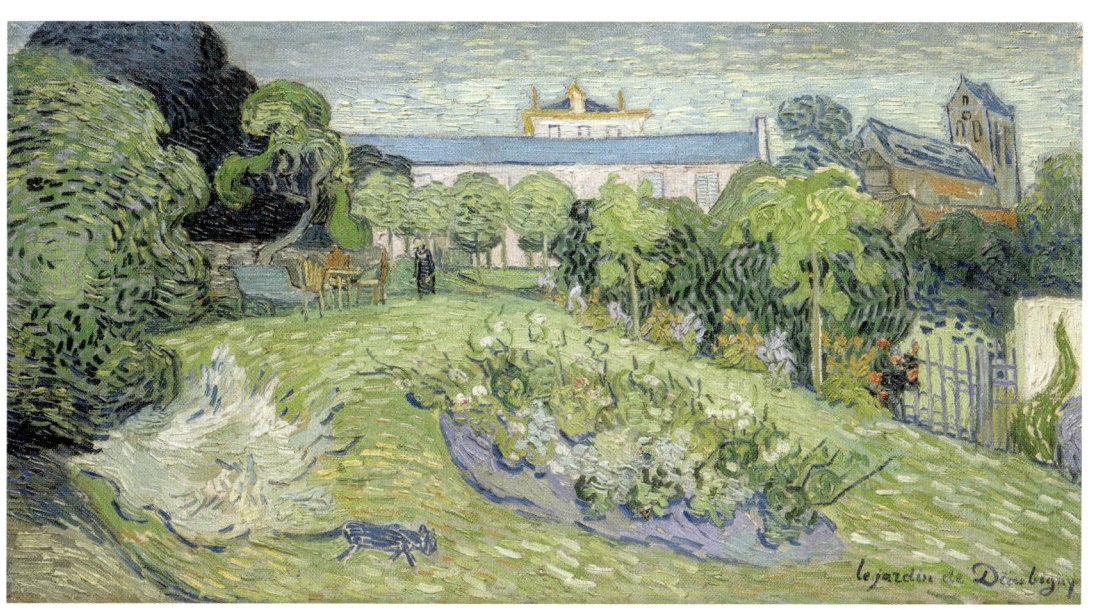

FURTHER READING

Bailey, Martin: *Studio of the South: Van Gogh in Provence*, London, 2016

Bakker, Nienke, and Coquery, Emmanuel, and van Tilborgh, Louis (authors): *Van Gogh in Auvers-sur-Oise: His Final Months*, Amsterdam, 2023

Bakker, Nienke, and Jansen, Leo, and Luijten, Hans (eds.): vangoghletters.org/vg/letters [letters from Vincent van Gogh online in English translations], accessed on Monday, 22. April 2024

Childs, Elizabeth C. (ed.): *Vincent van Gogh and the Painters of the Petit Boulevard*, New York, 2001

Groom, Gloria (ed.): *Van Gogh's Bedrooms*, New Haven, 2016

Hulsker, Jan: *The New Complete Van Gogh: Paintings, Drawings, Sketches*, Amsterdam, 1996

Kendall, Richard: *Van Gogh and Nature*, New Haven, 2015

Stein, Susan Alyson: *Van Gogh's Cypresses*, ex.cat., The Metropolitan Museum of Art, New York, 2023

Van Kooten, Toos: *The Paintings of Vincent van Gogh in the Collection of the Kröller-Müller Museum*, Otterlo, 2003

PHOTO CREDITS